The *Voice* That Changed Everything

The *Voice* That Changed Everything

A Book of Gratitude

TRACEE RANDALL & CAROL NEAL

The Voice That Changed Everything

ISBN: 978-0-9967975-1-1

Published by:
Atlanta Business Spotlight

Contents

Foreword

Bonnie Ross-Parker

I'm honored to have the opportunity to contribute my thoughts to this powerful publication, and thank Carol Neal and Tracee Randall for the opportunity. I have known these two dynamic women for several years, and it has been a pleasure to watch them grow and find success, and to see them create a new business venture, Atlanta Business Spotlight, which is helping so many people move forward personally and professionally.

This book collaboration is just one part of their new vision, and I love that they have chosen "The Voice That Changed Everything" as its theme. I know

the experiences shared by this group of authors concerning the people who have made a difference in their own lives will have a profound effect on our readers. As an author myself, I understand the impact of words. My career has been motivated and inspired throughout my personal and professional journey in large part because of the books I have read. There are many lessons I've learned and shared with others along the way. There were also a wide variety of situations I've had which left significant imprints on my life.

It's been over two decades since what I'm about to share actually happened. I was in the very early stages of my network marketing experience. At the time, given that I was a college graduate and had many years of business success to my credit, I looked at this new venture like 'a walk in the park'. Network marketing seemed so easy compared to teaching, franchising, publishing, etc. You talk about your company. You meet people, you might even invite them to join your organization. You do some training and reap the financial rewards. Sounds simple, right? That certainly was not my experience!

My efforts were disastrous. Looking back, I did a lot of talking and a lot of telling/selling. I thought for sure my own experience was persuasive enough to win others over. After all, in my business career I had sold 25 franchises for over $50K each. Why was my network marketing effort so difficult considering all that I had previously accomplished? I simply didn't have an answer. I became frustrated and discouraged, and I was very close to quitting.

I finally mustered the courage to share my experiences with my sponsor. She listened without interruption. She then asked me several questions.

"When was the last time you read a book specifically to expand your personal or professional development skills?"

"When you were in college, were you taught how to share about the network marketing industry?"

"Do you think people buy when you want them to, or when they are ready to purchase what you have to offer?"

Wow. She sure hit me head on with her feedback. At that time, I was not an avid reader of personal or business related books. I had not previously experienced the unique techniques and strategies necessary to be a successful network marketer. And, lastly, it never occurred to me that people would not want what I was selling! I thought everyone would see what I saw and want what I had.

This experience and conversation happened in November, 1995, and what followed had and continues to have a major impact on my life. Lorna Rasmussen looked me in the eye and asked me if I was ready to quit or do whatever was necessary to remain committed. She then said the following: (This is *the voice that changed everything* for me.) "I believe in you." The four words Lorna delivered that day offered a powerful and emotional message, one I have held close to my heart for 20 years.

At that time I was 51. Previously, I can't recall anyone who actually encouraged me the way she did that day. Her belief in me and the sincerity she demonstrated changed everything. I told her I was committed. I told her I was willing to read and learn and exhibit the highest level of integrity in the future.

I have kept that commitment in the years that followed. I only disengaged when the company changed direction and focus. I had achieved a high level of success by listening, trusting and believing I could be successful. Lorna was right. To achieve success in network marketing, you must establish relationships that go well beyond telling/selling.

The great news is that by listening to Lorna, following her advice and allowing her to serve as my mentor, I have had the good fortune of imparting that knowledge in others throughout the years that followed. First I had to believe in myself. I had to accept being worthy of success. Once I felt deserving, I felt compelled to share what I had learned and instill the same belief in other people I met—"You can do this." "You have what it takes." "You are awesome." "I believe in you." And to this day, that's how I've established and maintained relationships.

Not long ago I came across a beautiful document by author Kibi Yamada. I retyped it, laminated it and posted it on the cabinet above my computer. I hope it will give you the same encouragement that it continues to offer me:

Believe:
The start to a better world is our belief that it is possible.
Believe in your dreams.
Believe in today.
Believe that you are loved.
Believe that you make a difference.
Believe we can build a better world.
Believe when others might not.
Believe there's a light at the end of the tunnel.
Believe that you might be that light for someone else.
Believe that the best is yet to be.

Believe in each other.
Believe in yourself.
I believe in you.

As you reflect on *'the voice that changed everything'* for you, know that you also have a voice that has the power to change someone else. We all have moments throughout our lives to be 'the voice'—to care, to express gratitude, to show compassion, to listen and to make a difference. Leave positive, indelible imprints everywhere you go and in everything you do. People are watching what you do and listening to what you say. Believe in yourself. And, believe in the power you have to create a better world.

Editor's Note

David Bossen

When Tracee Randall asked me to edit this book, I saw it as an academic exercise. Editing is a job, and I was prepared. What I was not prepared for was the depth and breadth of life situations I encountered as I read these stories. We all know that every person has a story to tell. What we tried to capture in this book was a range of human experience, everything from death and tragedy to the triumph of love, family and faith.

Some of these stories will bring tears to your eyes. Others will make you nod in recognition of situations we are all familiar with. Others will demonstrate how faith in God can make all the difference as you navigate your way through difficult situations.

What is common to all these stories is the human element, where average people rise up to meet the challenges of life with humor, class and faith. These stories are deeply personal, yet they are about all of us. I hope you enjoy them as much as I did.

Introduction

Tracee Randall

Along my journey of self-development I have met some amazing people who have inspired me to be the very best that I can be. I began to think about all of the people who had stepped into my life and spoke words over me that allowed me to walk into the destiny that God intended for me, and I was overwhelmed with gratitude. How could I properly thank them? As I began to ask others about their journey, we all had a common thread, there was someone who believed in us even when we did not.

For all the authors represented here, when you read their stories of triumph, you will be inspired by their courage and their commitment to become the person they were destined to be. What we also noticed was that with each author who contributed here, they understand the power of the spoken word, the power of speaking *life* into others! For many of us, it was difficult to pinpoint just one person, as with most of us there are many voices that come along in our journey, some just for a season, some for a lifetime!

The purpose of this work is to acknowledge and thank in a powerful way those *voices* who impacted our lives. The Voice That Changed Everything is a book of gratitude! This book will inspire YOU to think about your own journey—and perhaps to go back and thank that person (or those people) who because of them, you are who you are!! We hope that as you read about how these incredible people have brought inspiration into the lives of our authors, YOU will be encouraged to think about who YOU can inspire! Who needs to hear YOUR VOICE?

One of my life's dreams has been to write a book. In March of 2015 I met two men who gave me the courage to step out in faith and write. Sometimes it just takes one word, one comment from someone and everything changes. I will never forget the first phone conversation that I had with Jim Britt and Jim Lutes at the beginning of this year. Their words, although I am sure they do not remember them, are forever etched into *my* mind, and their confirmation that I am a writer gave me the courage to move forward! I want to thank them both for including me as one of the co-authors in the book series, "The Change—Insights Into Self-Empowerment"—it was this opportunity that gave me the courage to write several books, including this one! It has been their on-going support and marketing advice that has helped my business partner Carol Neal and me create successful businesses and collaborations, such as this book, and we are grateful!

For all of us there are many people who helped make us who we are—for you it may be a friend, or a teacher, or a relative. It could have been a pastor or a business partner. Maybe it was a coach or counselor. Who saw greatness in you and helped you develop it? Who reached down to help you when you most needed it? Who has been the most powerful voice in YOUR life? It's time to thank them! This book is dedicated to the voices in our lives that mattered the most!

After reading this inspiring work you will want to say "thank you" to your *voice*! Carol and I will be giving you that opportunity as we continue our journey to inspire! We want to meet your VOICE!!

Carol D. Neal

Carol Neal's motto is "Let Your Light Shine". She is passionate about providing opportunities, resources and connections to help other people succeed. She learned this giving attitude from her Voice, her father, Larry Dressler, who lived his life in Christian service to others.

Carol was employed by Equifax for 25 years and was named to their Winner's Circle for her work in corporate training. She holds several certifications in the credit industry, has served on the Board of Directors for the Credit Education Resources Foundation and as International President of Credit Professionals International. She was named International Credit Professional

of the Year in 2007. She is a Certified True Colors Facilitator, a Certified Personal Life Coach, a Certified Public Speaker and a published author.

She started her own company in 2007 and has added several direct sales lines to her portfolio since then, including Reliv International and Organo. She is an avid networker and promoter, and has been an Xperience Connections leader for over six years. In 2015 she co-founded the Atlanta Business Spotlight with long-time business partner and friend Tracee Randall with the goal of giving others a platform to succeed. Carol resides in Alpharetta, GA where she is a full-time caregiver for her 92 year-old mother.

Contact Carol:

Carol@AtlantaBusinessSpotlight.com
www.facebook.com/shinewithcarol
www.letyourlightshine.myorganogold.com
www.twitter.com/NCDNeal
www.linkedin.com/in/letyourlightshine

The Voice That Made Me Everything

Carol D. Neal

OK, I admit it. I was a Daddy's girl. It probably had something to do with being the last of three daughters over a 20 year period. His first daughter was married with a girl of her own by the time I came along and his second daughter, who is 15 years older than me, was also almost out of the house, so I was pretty much raised as a single child. I wasn't born until Dad and my Mom (his third wife) had been married for 9 years, so I think he felt I was his last chance to have a 'chip off the old block'. I grew up learning how to drive boats, fish, ride motorcycles, play musical instruments, and eventually, fly a plane. These were all things that Dad enjoyed. I actually had the best of both worlds, because I was also very close to my Mom. She became my best friend in my teen years, and still is to this day, but we were a tight little three-some and I always remained close to my Dad. It is his voice that shaped my perceptions of the world and, more importantly, my perceptions of myself. This is the story of how he did that, with his words and by example, from my first breath to his last.

Lawrence F. Dressler (Larry to his friends, and everyone was a friend to Dad) always expected a lot out of me. He always bragged about me to the outside world, even when I felt I wasn't living up to his expectations. I was his "right hand girl" (i.e. unpaid employee) much of the time. Dad was a top notch appraisal engineer. He traveled around the US appraising companies and plants that were offered for sale, making note of every piece of equipment and inventory down to the last brad. I know, because I helped him review and determine prices on those lists. I loved every moment I got to spend with him in our home office doing "grown up work". When he had something interesting to appraise, like the Toledo Blade newspaper, a light bulb factory, or an ice cream plant down in Florida, he would get permission to take me out of school on a "field trip," where I got to tour the facilities and see their inner workings, in exchange for reporting back to my class on what I'd seen.

Dad didn't have to tell me to give back to the community and to always do my best, because he SHOWED me that was the way to be every day. I also helped him over the years with committee reports and membership lists for the Benevolent Order of Elks Lodge and the Fraternal Order of Police Association and other organizations he was involved in. Dad was always in the thick of things and usually in charge. He was a charter member and Commander of the Minnetonka Power Squadron, a member of the Aircraft Owners and Pilots Association, a deacon and steward in his church, president of his homeowners association, and a frequent community service award winner...from a radio Good Neighbor Award of the Northwest to a Meritorious Service

Award from the Advisory Committee on Water Recreation in Lake County, Florida.

Dad would sacrifice anything for me and Mom. When I was just a pre-teen, he stood in line outdoors for HOURS in freezing winter conditions in Cleveland, Ohio, to get us tickets for an Elvis Presley concert. While Dad was an accomplished musician himself, he was not a particularly big fan of Elvis, but he knew that I was. (I've always been a little out of sync...I fell in love with Elvis when my friends were crazy about Bobby Sherman and David Cassidy.) Dad wanted to surprise me by taking me to that concert, and he was determined to get those tickets despite the wait and the snow. I can still remember the electricity that ran through the audience when Elvis came out on stage. Mom and Dad and I were sitting in the highest seats in the auditorium as far away from stage as we could be, but that didn't matter, because you could feel Elvis' charismatic energy crackle around the room the moment he stepped on stage! And I also felt the love of a father who would make that kind of sacrifice of his time and money and comfort to make someone else's dream come true.

Dad was my "Knight in Shining Armor", and my protector. He taught me to ride motorcycles at a young age, and one of my first bikes was a little black Harley 90cc. I was proudly scooting along on it next to him on his big "matching" Harley Full Dress Black Leather Hog on our way to get my license, when a car swerved into our lane and made me stall out. After making sure I was not hurt, Dad took off after the driver, pulled him over and chewed him out...in full Daddy Bear mode!

But Dad also let me spread my wings, encouraging me to try theatre, art and music. I took part in church trips that included a life changing four weeks volunteering in Great Britain and

Scotland the summer before my senior year in high school, as well as local outings where we did volunteer work in our own community and in the inner-city. He taught me to swim and dive, even though I was scared of the water, and to make an effort to meet new people and make friends everywhere I went, even though I was shy.

Dad was a songwriter, a poet and a romantic...and a sensitive man. I still remember the tears in his eyes the first time I got glasses as a little girl. As we left the doctor's office, I said, "Oh, Daddy, look… I can see the individual leaves on that tree." Until then he never realized that my world up to that point had just been vague shapes, and he broke down and cried.

Dad was always proud of me and encouraged me to take "center stage"...which explains a lot for those who know me now! When I was still in diapers, I was featured in several films he made on water safety for the Power Squadron. He encouraged me to start a neighborhood newspaper when I was ten years old. In his eyes I could do anything, and sometimes his strong belief in me got me into trouble.

For example, when he and Mom dropped me off for a week at a Camp Fire Girls camp, he bragged about me to the counselor, telling her how I was out on the Cuyahoga River when I was just one week old, and could handle boats with outboard and inboard twin engines. That backfired on me when, the next day, she put me in charge of two other girls in a canoe due to my "experience" with boats. Need I say that I had never been in a canoe before in my life? The first time out ended up with three very wet little girls!

I've always felt I had a low tolerance for pain (as in I was a big baby), so I was shocked to hear my father tell the doctors at the Cleveland Clinic, as I was having tests for undiagnosed stomach problems, that there must be something seriously wrong because HIS little girl had an extremely high pain threshold and NEVER complained. From that day forward, I tried to live up to that belief.

Whenever I won an award or achieved a goal, Dad was there to tell the world. Sometimes that was embarrassing. As an adult, I did a lot of traveling for my employer, Equifax, helping to train the field office personnel on how to handle automated customer data, and Equifax also supported me very generously in our trade association, sending me to conferences all over the US and Canada. I remember being mortified when I learned that Dad was telling everyone back home that the company was sending me everywhere to get all of their offices "in line" and to teach them how to do things right. Looking back now, I know he just believed in me and was proud of his "little girl".

I did always want to make him proud. One of his fondest wishes was for me to follow him in the air. He had been in the Army Air Corps and was a private pilot and it was just "understood" that I would take lessons and solo when I was 16. I actually wasn't that keen on the idea...I enjoyed flying, but I realized that there was an awful lot of work, and a lot of math involved (which I hate) to becoming a pilot. But when I was introduced to my very cute and hunky young flight instructor, I decided to give it a try, and I did solo on my 16th birthday. The first touch and go landing was great....smooth and perfectly aligned. I think I was concentrating so hard on everything I had to do that it didn't quite sink in that I was in the plane by myself. The second one got a little shaky... sometime during that second go-around it dawned on me that it really was just me up in the air. Still, I could hear my Dad's voice saying "you can do it", and I went around for my third landing, and bounced all over the runway! But you know the saying…any landing you can walk away from is a good one!

I went up a couple more times by myself after that, but it was enough for me to realize I just wasn't comfortable in the air by myself. I loved flying co-pilot for Dad, taking the controls many times, enjoying the view and the company and quiet time together, but knowing that he had the ultimate responsibility for getting us where we needed to be. I couldn't enjoy the EXPERIENCE of flying when I was the only one responsible for everything that went into the ACT of flying. It was one of the first times I knew I was going to consciously disappoint Dad…but he reasoned that at least he had a skilled co-pilot that knew what she was doing in the case of an emergency. He also had bragging rights about having a daughter that soloed on the day she turned 16. He never made me feel like a quitter when I didn't take my lessons any further.

In a way, I was able to make it up to him later by bringing a special person into his life. Dad practically adopted my high school boyfriend, and Dad was the one who encouraged him to learn to fly. My friend was the one that followed in Dad's footsteps, eventually flying as a Major in the West Virginia Air National Guard in Iraq, Kuwait and Saudia Arabia, and later as a commercial pilot. He became a lifetime friend and Dad's "almost son", and was another example of a person who was changed forever because of Dad's voice.

When it was time for me to pick a college, I won a National Merit Scholarship from a school I had never heard of…Mississippi University for Women. I was considering several schools but Dad flew us down to visit that one in February. The girls welcomed us with their soft Southern accents, and the grounds people were cutting the grass there at the same time it was snowing in Cincinnati and Michigan, which were my other two choices. So, even though it was incredibly far away from home and a whole new culture for me, there was no contest when it came to my decision. (The scholarship didn't hurt, either.) Once again, my father's voice told me that I could do it. I met my husband in college (someone had the brilliant idea of putting an Air Force Training Base next to a girl's school) and we eloped. It disappointed my parents greatly when I left school in my second year, and Dad never got along well with my husband even though they also had airplanes in common. My husband was a mechanic in the Air Force and then went to work for Delta, which is how we ended up in Atlanta. We didn't see my parents a lot during the next 11 years. But when my marriage ended, my parents were there for me again, coming down to help me find a place to live, and shoring up my battered self-confidence.

My parents and I had many good times and trips as a family unit after that, and when they retired and moved to Florida, I was able to spend a lot of time with them there as well. I always had that strong sense of coming home and being loved unconditionally, and was still always encouraged that I could do and be whatever I desired. And there were new neighbors and friends that had to hear all about Daddy's little girl and all her accomplishments…he was once again my strongest cheerleader, that voice that said I could do anything. I realize now that what Dad was doing was edifying me. Ironically, edification is now an integral part of all of my businesses. It's just one more way that Dad's voice helped make me the person I am today.

When Dad developed Alzheimer's, it was my turn to be the voice for him. His condition left him with a personality-altering case of paranoia and delusions, and this once amazingly strong man who had overflowed with good humor and Christian love became suspicious and afraid and difficult to live with...it got to the point where he could not be left alone. When he developed Sundown Syndrome everything escalated, the agitation and confusion would worsen as the daylight faded. Mother was the epitome of patience and grace under pressure and gave him constant love and care, but too many times it was the disease that responded to her, not the man who I know still loved her deeply.

This man who had made a friend of every stranger started pushing loved ones away. But thankfully, I was still "Daddy's girl". He always recognized me and welcomed me and trusted me. He trusted me to make sure he got the right care when he was in the hospital or in a rehab facility, and he trusted me to handle the financial decisions. He trusted me to take care of Mom, and to move them up to Georgia when she needed my help with him. And on that last day in hospice when he was taking his last breaths, and he was worried that he hadn't done enough for his heavenly reward, I was the voice that prayed with him and reassured him that he had done more than enough because he'd been a blessing to so many, and I could see the relief and gratitude in his eyes, and a hint of the smile of the man that he had been, before those eyes closed forever.

This is the letter that Dad wrote to me when I left Ohio in 1976 for my first year at the "W", and I think you will hear the special voice that always believed in me and loved me unconditionally. I love you Dad, and miss you every day. Thank you for being the voice that encouraged me to believe in myself, and made me the woman I am today who now has a mission to help others believe in themselves as well!

Dear Carol:

Oh where has the summer gone?
The weather's so rainy and cool.
Where has our little girl gone?
Grown up and off to school.

It seems like only yesterday
We were walking round the bend
Talking, laughing and arguing some
About the school you would attend.

We all knew MUW was far, far away
But—just like the summer heat
I wasn't going to miss you—<u>not</u> <u>much</u>
Or at least not <u>right</u> away!

But then I forgot how cool the fall can be....
How barren the ground...the empty look
When the leaves depart the trees.
Sure, there's color now and then—pretty things to see...
But I'm afraid my thoughts
Wander back to summer—you, Mom and me.

Well, it won't always be rainy and cool
It will be colder with ice and snow.
Then I'll know where summers really go...
With Carol...way down South at school!

So in the cool and cold days ahead
Keep us lonely ones up here
A little warmer with your
Letters and messages of good cheer.

Fall's here, winter will come and go,
Then spring, exciting, not so cool.
I'll be looking forward to summer
And Carol back home from school.

Tracee Randall

Success in business comes easily for entrepreneur Tracee Randall. In the last 31 years, she and her husband Bobby, have built million-dollar corporations in the service and relocation industries.

Success with her health and self-image did not come as easy, and it is that journey that she shares here...the journey from a young girl with eating disorders and panic attacks, to the healthy, confident success transformation coach and public speaker she is today.

Tracee is a sought after speaker, addressing women's groups across the country about overcoming food addiction

and self-esteem issues, and she has several published works in women's magazines. She is an author in the best-selling book series, "The Change—Insights Into Empowerment" and she has recently released her first book, "The FASTest Way to God's Favor and Blessing."

She is considered by many to be Georgia's foremost Wellness

Coach, and has several workshops on the subject of wellness including "Get MAD About Cancer." She is recognized internationally as a speaker and works closely with the American Anti-Cancer Institute to educate families on the prevention of disease.

Her programs are designed to empower the entrepreneur as well as traditional businesses as she educates on team building, creating healthy relationships, and increasing profits from the sole proprietor to the large corporation. Audiences love her funny and entertaining style as she speaks boldly on every subject she attacks. Her workshops "Make Up Your Mind" and "H.A.T. Training—How to Attract Your Team" are designed to create strong goals and relationships that generate profits and change!

She is currently working on her book titled "Beneath The Veil" which will inspire women to break out of their shame and guilt and walk in the greatness that God has planned for them. You can read some of her excerpts on her blog located at TraceeRandall.com

Contact Tracee to speak at your convention, workshop, church group or company—go to her website for more information!

Contact Tracee:
Tracee@TraceeRandall.com
Facebook: Tracee Smith Randall
Instagram: tracee.randall
Website: TraceeRandall.com

Tracee's Voice

The Voice of Courage

Tracee Randall

In October 2014, Bobby and I celebrated our 30th wedding anniversary. Statistically, we should never have made it past the 1st year. Thank God we aren't a statistic.

On October 13, 1984, we got married in a small chapel in my hometown. As I walked down the aisle, with my wedding gown reflecting the candlelight, wearing a veil attached to a circle of orchids that my Mamaw had made, our eyes met and we both smiled as if this was the first day of the rest of our lives. But there was a secret hiding beneath that veil that sunny afternoon. As I walked down the aisle and looked into the eyes of the man I was about to marry, even then I knew that his voice of courage would change everything for me. And even then I was very grateful for it. Looking back, I never had any doubt that I would be happily married to the person who would become my best friend, but I know he did!!

Our fairytale love story wasn't in reality either one—at least not up to that point. It was more of a romance novel gone bad, and we were the players in the "made-for-TV" movie. That day, October 13, 1984, we were strangers, woven together by a secret. A secret that I made him promise to keep, a lie that should have caused our marriage to end in divorce. But somehow, by God's grace, it continued in love instead.

It's every girl's dream to be swept off her feet by a "knight in shining armor", and I was no exception. Yes, Bobby Randall, my husband of 30 years (as of the date of writing this—June, 2015) is the voice that changed everything for me. He is my best friend, my hero, my protector, the priest of our home, the father of our amazing sons...the man who married me when I was scared and frightened, ashamed and hurting. He trusted me when others told him I was not to be trusted. And he refused to abandon me, in spite of being told that I was unworthy of love.

In the summer of 1984, I lived in a college community and, having just graduated with a teaching degree in English Education the December before, I realized that I had outgrown my small town. I needed to re-create my life and decided to move back to Dallas, Texas, where I had grown up.

I had struggled for as long as I could remember with self-esteem issues, self-hate and food addictions that controlled my life. Every waking moment was consumed with fear and panic—emotions that I had learned to hide very well behind a glass of wine and a bigger-than-life laugh. Somehow, by being the center of attention, by laughing the loudest and smiling the broadest, I hid my fears and hurt. More than anything, I desired the love of a man. I read way too many romance novels growing up, and I had no role models in my life to teach me the true meaning of love between a man and a woman. I mistook sex for love and believed the lie that physical love could satisfy.

By August of 1984, I had hit rock bottom. I hated myself more than ever, but I had enough sense to know that if I continued to hang around my present environment, nothing would change.

What I am about to tell you hurts me more than any other part of this story, but I know that my willingness to share my truth will *set others free*. I have NEVER shared this with anyone else, not even Bobby, and it explains the depth of my hurt, the extent of my pain, and the length of time I suffered.

At the age of 25, I had been taking birth control pills since I was 12 years old. I had spent the previous 13 years feeling worthless and used, lying to my parents, and lying to myself. I spent 13 years praying for God to bring me a man who would love ME—not my body—but ME…the "little girl" Tracee. By June of 1984, I had decided this man did not exist. That summer, I realized that I had lost my identity and that I had to make a change, or I would not be able to continue living. I was mentally defeated and worn out, and DETERMINED to start over somehow.

So, my decision to sell everything I owned, say goodbye to my past and start over in a new but familiar city was my plan of salvation. I promised myself that I would not fall into the weakness of having sex again until I met a man who truly loved me. In my sick, twisted, hurting mind, throwing away my birth control pills was the only way to ensure I would not be tempted, since my biggest fear was getting pregnant.

The next couple of weeks were spent preparing to make the move, to make the CHANGE. In spite of my intense loneliness, I had a lot of friends, and they rallied around me as I planned my new life. The week before my "take off" was filled with parties and farewell dinners. The "big party" was planned five days before my little red Cavalier was scheduled to make the five-hour trip to Dallas, packed with all my worldly belongings. It was at that party that everything changed. It was there that my destiny would be written, and my true CHANGE would begin.

I would like to tell you it was "love at first sight," but that would be a lie, so I will go deeper beneath the "veil," pushing all my guilt and pride aside. We were not friends, but Bobby and I had known *of* each other. He played water volleyball every weekend at the apartment pool where we both lived, and quite frankly, I didn't really like him. He was loud and obnoxious (well I am being "real") and always drunk, and I never had any reason to talk to him.

That night, he walked into my kitchen as I was making my third batch of frozen margaritas, and started flirting shamelessly with me. Tequila is the enemy of good intention, and by midnight I found myself lying next to him, full of guilt, hurt and self-hatred for my weakness. In spite of the fact that I had just stopped using birth control pills, I believed I was "safe" from pregnancy, something that turned out to be a horrible miscalculation on my part.

Like the alcoholic who takes that sip and then justifies it by saying it will be his last, I continued to have sex with Bobby for the next 5 days, swearing to myself that this would be the last time I ever compromised myself for the sake of loneliness. Little did I know that I would be right, but not for reason you might expect!

Always the dreamer, always the optimist, always the romantic, I allowed myself to believe Bobby would fall in love with me, beg me to stay, and we would live happily ever after. But it wasn't to be. The night before my departure, I stood at his door, looked into his eyes, and silently begged him to stop me.

He didn't. I said things like, "You'll never find someone who will love you like I will," and I BELIEVED IT! I had so much love to give, but no love for myself. He watched me walk away and, though I felt defeated, I was a SURVIVOR. With each step I took toward my already packed car, I raised my head taller and stronger, and I decided that, somehow, I would find my destiny. Silent, hot tears stung my cheeks as I bravely walked away, still listening for words that never came, still hoping he would not let me go.

The next few weeks in Dallas were a whirlwind. I unloaded my car into my new apartment, and started my new life. It was like a surreal dream. I found a job doing what I knew best, and that was cocktail waitressing. It was quick, easy money.

I was 25 and tired. I had worked to support myself since I was 14, and had watched my single mom waste her life chasing the dream of a good man. She held down three jobs, but still barely made ends meet. Instead of sleeping, she would lie in bed night at night, reading romance novels about a fictional heroine rescued by an elusive prince.

I felt like I had already worked and lived a lifetime, and I was bone tired. I came home in the early morning hours after a long shift and threw my wadded tip money onto the floor. I sank down into my plastic pool chair, my only furniture, and drank wine by the gallon until I cried myself to sleep. I was lonelier than ever.

I wrote love letters to Bobby; long, funny, witty letters that poured out of my soul, all the while praying that he would realize his love for me and come rescue this damsel in distress. He called me, and we spent hours talking about nothing, just wasting time. We were too far apart for it to matter. He promised to come to Dallas, and take me out for a night on the town.

I drank glass after glass of cheap white wine mixed with sprite and ice, and cried my way through another 10-page letter, until I finally passed out, pen in hand.

Three more weeks went by, and my days consisted mostly of recovering from cheap wine hangovers by the swimming pool. In the evenings, I strapped on my high heels and racked up impressive tips by serving drinks to drunks. Although I had my share of the inevitable flirtatious attempts to lure me into a bedroom, and in spite of my severe depression and loneliness, I held firm. I was determined to change, and each night I went home by myself, where I unloaded more wads of crumpled bills from my apron pocket, stripped out of my cocktail attire, and climbed into the "safety" of my pajamas.

It was then I realized that something was terribly wrong. I had missed my period. At first, I laughed it off, thinking it was impossible, as I had not been with anyone since I left Bobby and I had calculated that I was "safe" during those days with him. Just to be sure, I went to a drug store and purchased a pregnancy test that contained two test kits. I took the first test, and nervously waited. Fifteen minutes later, the test came back positive, and the biggest fear of my life had become a reality. I tested again, just to be sure, with the same result. I was pregnant, and I was in a panic.

I am the one who jumps out of the plane and figures out how to build a parachute on the way down. I am the cat that is thrown across the room and lands on his feet, only to go back shamelessly for another throw. True to form, my mind began to plan my response. Plan A, Plan B—I always had a plan.

I gathered all my tip money and booked a flight back home for the next weekend. I called Bobby and told him I would be there for a few days, and wanted to see him. My resolve never wavered as I devised my plan. He would marry me in two weeks, in a church, with rings and dresses and bridesmaids and all the "bells and whistles!" My family could not know! Plan A was complete. Over the next few days, I rehearsed every detail, while nervously looking down at my hard, flat stomach, wondering about the changes to come. There was no more alcohol consumed from that point on. I might have been irresponsible, but I wasn't stupid!

Abortion. Adoption. Both options were suggested by my well-meaning friends when I told them the news. Neither option was acceptable to me.

I worked on a backup Plan B, just in case. I would pack my few belongings and drive out west somewhere. I would find a shelter or program that would help me and I would raise my baby alone. I would run away. My family would never know. I would simply disappear.

To be honest, I never really worked through all the details of that plan, because Plan A was the only real option in my mind. I would have to swallow my pride and persuade Bobby to marry me, and "save face" with my family.

It was the thought of my Mamaw finding out what happened that worried me. My sweet Mamaw, who thought I "hung the moon," who had helped me through college, who thought I was a "good girl." It was her reaction I feared the most.

I was motivated by pride and shame, even during a time when it was considered normal for unmarried people to live together and have sex and have babies. I was *not* one of "those" people. No one in my family could know.

After ordering dinner, and declining an offer for wine or a margarita, I summoned the courage to tell Bobby the true purpose of the trip. You could see the news sink into him, as the smile left his face. The mood shifted, and I saw the distrust in his eyes. But I was prepared. I had rehearsed the scene over and over, covering every angle. I explained how I KNEW he was the father (that statement sounds so cold and sad, even today), and waited for him to react. He suggested that we go home and think it over. "What is there to think about?" I wanted to scream. But instead, I smiled and agreed. When we left that night, I knew he was scared and confused. Who wouldn't be?

I had laid the plan out perfectly for Bobby, giving him the exact steps we would take to ensure my secret was safe from my family. I told him that if he was not willing to follow it exactly, I would leave and he would NEVER hear from me again. He would NEVER see or know his child. I meant it with every fiber of my being. I also believed with all my heart that I would be the most amazing wife Bobby could ever hope for, and that we could, and would, live "happily ever after." In spite of it all I still believed in fairy tales.

The next two days were more than miserable. I wanted to scream out, "Help me, I'm pregnant and scared," but instead I laughed and chit-chatted with old friends about nothing. As word got around that I was pregnant, more unsolicited advice came from all angles—mostly advocating abortion or adoption—neither of which was acceptable. I had enough exposure to church teachings to fear God's punishment for killing a child, and the maternal instinct that this little person would count on me, and would LOVE me unconditionally argued against adoption.

Bobby was burdened by this situation. He did not trust me, for good reason, and the advice he was receiving from all his friends was "Run as fast as you can!" Meanwhile, I was called nasty names like "slut" (and worse), but in my heart I didn't believe that label applied to me. I knew WHY I did what I did. I *knew* it was out of fear and hopelessness. If that's what it means to be a slut, then I guess they were right. Even so, I forgave myself.

I was preparing to return to Dallas, and still had not heard from Bobby. I began formulating Plan B more clearly, as Bobby was moving too slowly and my pride was starting to rise up. I was done taking advice, and having people feel sorry for me. I escaped to the parking lot of the apartment complex, and spent the night curled up in the front seat of the rental car, out of money and out of hope.

I was awakened by a gentle knock on the car window. I jerked myself up, realizing it was morning. Bobby was standing quietly by the car, with tears streaming down his cheeks. I rolled the window down and looked at his sad and tired face. I could see the torment written in his expression. He whispered, "I will marry you, Tracee. In spite of all my friends' advice, and my fear of all of this, my biggest fear is that I would have a son and never know him, or a daughter and never hold her hand." It was a voice of courage. By now I was crying too, and I opened the door and rushed to him. We stood outside in the hot morning sun, crying and hugging, and praying that everything would be okay.

That moment alone would make Bobby the "voice that changed everything" for me. But there is so much more. So many days of learning to love each other. So many days of laughing together, watching Robby (our son) grow. So many nights of lying side by side, talking deep into the night.

Now, family albums line our walls, floor to ceiling, all precious memories of our incredible adventure together! A lifetime of miracles. We raised two incredible sons, and now have three amazing grandchildren. We came to know the Lord together. We pray together, and we serve in ministries in our church.

30 years have passed since I walked down that aisle, a secret tucked deep inside my heart—one of shame and guilt—not just of the baby that grew inside of me, but of the lies I had told myself that I was unworthy of love. Today, almost 31 years later, with a gray beard and speckles of gray scattered in his hair, he is still beside me, supporting me. He sacrifices every day to give me the freedom to write, and to pursue the vision that God has put inside of me. He stands strong, and allows me to share my story, this story. He knows that by sharing my experience, other women will be set free to forgive themselves. Even today he is the VOICE that speaks greatness into me and laughs when I laugh and cries when I cry. He is strong when I am weak, and he loves me with all his heart. He encourages me. He believes in me. He forgives me. He is always my voice of courage, my voice of hope. He loves me. He is my VOICE.

Laura B. Baker

Laura B Baker is a wife and mother of 5 amazing people. She enjoys her family and helping others see the HOPE that surrounds them. She is dedicated to showing, both adults and children, how to find the bright side and humor in any situation. The world is a better place when you smile, and it is her mission to make sure there are smiles everywhere she goes. Life is more pleasant with a smile and a good chuckle.

She works with children helping to teach them how to navigate through life with a positive attitude and humor. It doesn't matter what the struggle, you can get through it with hard work and a lot of laughter. The bigger the challenge, the more laughter is needed.

As a Mindset Coach she is passionately encouraging people toward VICTORIOUS SUCCESS!

Recently she conquered her own inner demons and launched a social media video business. Everyone can become a superstar of their own life, and any business can generate buzz, get their name out to potential customers, and increase sales. PR4Profit boldly breathes life into your social media platforms.

Get in touch with Laura at (678) 696-1594 or pr4profit@gmail.com, follow her on Twitter @laurabbaker, and on Facebook as LauraBBaker. Visit her website www.LauraBBaker.info

Laura's Voice

The Trail Blazer

Laura B. Baker

What do Walt Disney, Steve Jobs, and Bill Gates have in common? What about Cher, Tom Cruise, and Whoopi Goldberg? You may not know this, but Thomas Edison, Alexander G. Bell, and Albert Einstein all had it too. Muhammad Ali, Will Smith, and Michael J. Fox. The list is long and distinguished. Even John F. Kennedy and Winston Churchill were one of us. Steven Spielberg was diagnosed when he was 60. What is the common thread running through each of us? What is it that makes us different?

It is an elite club. Membership is costly and can be very painful, yet those of us who are members could not be who we are without it.

Like a lot of daughters, I was a daddy's girl. He was the smartest man I have ever known. His math skills were legendary throughout the family, and within our circle of friends. He earned two degrees from Georgia Tech. He also received a patent from the U. S. government for something he invented while working for AT&T. I was so proud to be his daughter, and that remains true to this day. The smartest thing he ever did, in my humble opinion, was marry my mom.

Laura Helen Hadaway, better known as Mama to me, was born on Easter Sunday at Grady Memorial Hospital in Atlanta, Georgia during the Great Depression. Because of health complications, three separate doctors strongly encouraged my grandparents to terminate the pregnancy. Thankfully they refused, and I'm here today to share just how extraordinary a person she became.

I don't know if it was growing up during the depression and the war to end all wars (WWII), coming from the first class of students to attend 12 years of school (the class of '51), being part of the first group of kids to be called 'teenagers," or working, as a teenager, at Lockheed typing the manuals for the B-1 bomber; but somewhere along the line she was destined to be a trail blazer and a non-conformist. She did this while maintaining her wicked wit and southern charm. I just learned recently that the Israeli army discovered a way to capture water out of the air. Big deal…Mama has been taking the condensation from her dehumidifier to water her plants for years. Proving, yet again, she is ahead of the curve.

My parents became acquainted with each other growing up. They lived in the small town of Marietta, Georgia. My grandfathers played chess every week, and my grandmothers were in the same Sunday School class for over 50 years. So when the phone call (for the first date) from "Bobby Bevers" came, Mama thought he was calling for her older sister (they were in the same class at school). Bobby the quiet introvert was drawn to Mama's charisma and charm like a moth to a flame. They dated while Daddy was in college and Mama was still in high school.

Upon graduating from Georgia Tech, Daddy got a job and moved to Chicago, IL. He was so far away, and Mama missed him terribly. She also felt he was dragging his feet in their relationship, so being the trail blazer that she was, she took matters into her own hands and proposed to him on the old bridge hanging over the Chattahoochee River. She married very young, which wasn't so uncommon in those days, but they waited 5 years to begin having children. They wanted to have time together to build the lifelong friendship and marriage they enjoyed so much. You can say they made up for it though by having four children in five years; three boys and me, the only daughter.

Growing up, Mama loved to read and make up games to remember words. Her vocabulary is quite extensive. Little did she know how much her love for reading and all those word games would come to serve her later.

Raising four children can be very exciting. It is also very hard work. Entertaining the younger kids while the older kids are working on homework is challenging, to say the least. So imagine the energy required to undertake a massive assault against the educational establishment. This would require her biggest act of trail blazing yet, and it revolved around me.

If necessity is the mother of invention, then my mom and Thomas Edison were kindred spirits. Although Mama never invented anything, she certainly was every bit as creative as he was. She first realized there was something going on with me when I started school. With so many children, she didn't have time to question my lack of interest in reading. I had done well with the "ABC" song and all the other fun activities in Sunday School and preschool.

It wasn't until first grade that she began to see a problem emerge; a problem that would radically change my world forever. It seemed simple enough at the time, I would just need a little longer to learn how to read. Each week I would bring home the list of new words that I was required to learn to read and spell. My mom would patiently point to a word on the list and inevitably I would say the wrong word. Although it was always one of the words on the list, I would rarely pick the correct one. Week after week, month after month, mom and I would do this dance.

She could not understand my inability to sound out the words or identify the words properly. She had conferences with my teachers and administrators, and everyone agreed I was intelligent, still, I just couldn't put the letters together to recognize the words. Math was also a challenge for me. As the daughter of a mathematical genius, it was clear to her something was amiss. She had become my advocate.

There is no telling how much time and energy Mama spent trying to find answers to the questions that were piling up. The only perspective I have is from my point of view, and the conversations we have had throughout the years. All I know is that it was difficult for me to read, and the older I got, the further behind I found myself compared to the rest of the kids in my class. By the time I was in second grade, Mama was on a crusade.

Unhappy with the answers from school administrators, she took it upon herself to find a solution. She began by doing her own investigation. A psychiatrist was brought in to help define the situation. She found that my IQ was 3 points below genius level, so intelligence wasn't the issue. Yet, my disability was so bad that I qualified for a program called "Reading for the Blind."

This, of course, made everything more perplexing. The psychiatrist who brought in to evaluate me spent what seemed to me to be several days testing for everything from mental illness to sheer stupidity. Although she acknowledged that I was extremely intelligent, she said I would never learn how to read, or drive a car. I would need a paid companion to help me navigate public transportation because I wouldn't know where to get off of the bus on my own. And as if this weren't bad enough, the psychiatrist also told my mother that if I were forced to try to learn how to read, I would rebel against my parents, hate them, and become an unwed teenage mother.

My mom, being the true southern lady she is, thanked the doctor, left the room and told me all she thought I needed to hear: that I had the highest IQ in our house and everything was going to work out.

There's no telling how the conversation with my dad went that evening because my mom and I have never discussed it, but I'm just guessing it was very interesting. Somewhere between that appointment and the rest of my life, my mom and dad decided that the psychiatrist was a quack. Mama was going to do everything within her power to ignore just about everything that woman told her.

By the time third grade was coming to an end, my father changed jobs, and our family moved from South Carolina to the great state of Georgia. All I know about the move was that Daddy got a better job, and we moved to one of the best school systems around. It didn't hurt that all of our family was about thirty minutes away, either.

Mom figured out from her research that I have Dyslexia, defined as "any of various reading disorders associated with impairment of the ability to interpret spatial relationships or to integrate auditory and visual information." That is Dictionary. com's way of saying I see words, letters, and numbers in strange ways and differing order. The TV show "60 Minutes" ran a segment about what it was like to have dyslexia. They placed an elaborate maze in front of a mirror. You would then try to find your way through the maze using only the reflected image as a visual cue to guide you to the finish line. The truth is, I don't have a clue whether that example was an accurate representation or not, but I can tell you this: If there is a misprint in something I am reading, I get caught up in an endless loop until I figure it out. It can be quite amusing and infuriating.

Yes it is the dyslexia, or learning disability if you prefer, that puts me in the elite group with Bruce Springsteen and the aforementioned people above. Knowing that I was in such company would have changed many things for me growing up. Reading for a dyslexic is very labored. It is a constant battle with your eyes and brain. You're never quite sure if you are seeing what is on the paper or some image your brain is using to mess up your day.

The best way I can think of to torture a dyslexic student would be when your well-meaning teacher says "we're going down the row, and everybody needs to read a paragraph out loud." Where you are seated in the classroom determines how long you have to sit there knowing the utter shame and humiliation that is coming at you, and there is no way out! Every single person in that classroom is about to know just how stupid you are. They are all going to know that you are a dummy or some kind of idiot. There is no way to fake it and your deepest, darkest secret is going to be unveiled in front of your friends and peers. You can't read, and now everybody is going to know it. The older you get, the worse you feel.

When fifth grade rolled around I was shuffled from one special program to another. I went to the county reading center three days a week so I could work with a teacher whom, I would find out later, used our work sessions as research for her PhD. She was very nice to me, and I worked very hard when I was with her. We sat in a room with a great big mirror for our two hour sessions. I know now there were people and/or cameras behind the mirror, but I didn't know that at the time. There are movies (we call them videos now) of our time together, and I pray I never see any of them. I hope they were all destroyed by some natural disaster. Just thinking about it now makes me feel violated. Once again I was exposed, this time to strangers. I'll never know who saw those films. All I really remember is that I desperately wanted to please Mrs. Campbell, but I am not sure I ever did. Something good did come from that experience, however, I got to spend a lot of alone time with my mom (which is cherished when you are one of four kids) as she carted me back and forth each week.

Upon arrival back at school, I would either go to class with my peers, or I would go to another Special Ed class. I hated fifth grade, and I don't think Mama was any happier with it than I was. That may have been the year the principal said "Well look at her, she doesn't look retarded." Yes, my mom still feels nauseous when you mention that principal's name.

My poor mom drove me back and forth to the county reading center three days a week, and spent countless hours every day after school going over what I should have learned (her version of homeschool) at school. She also volunteered for every program she could find so I could get the help I needed during the weekends. All the while, she worked to keep my self-esteem at a manageable level, so I would be interested and motivated enough to continue the hard work. I was a dyslexic, not an idiot, and I wasn't getting it. Whatever the teachers were doing didn't seem to be working. I was not even close to grade level and it wasn't getting any better.

Then...something happened between 6th and 7th grade. I wanted to get my ears pierced. My mom, on the other hand, was against it. This was a typical argument between a mother and her almost teen daughter. It was the same argument time after time. She wasn't going to budge and neither was I. With four daughters of my own now, I realize that I must have driven Mama to the point of insanity.

Despite her feelings, and being the trail blazer that she was, she made a deal with me: if I could go the entire school year with all A's and B's, I could get my ears pierced at the end of the school year. I'm sure in her mind it was a low risk deal. The only A' and B's I had ever received were because the teachers liked me and felt sorry for me. I was going into 7th grade with the reading ability of a 2nd grader. Mama was quite confident that I would not be getting my ears pierced.

However, something else happened that year. The professionals were finally beginning to understand dyslexia. I was placed in an SLD (Specific Learning Disability) class with a teacher I LOVED! She was rocking. She was young, hip, and trained to work with kids like me. She challenged and inspired me. She made it fun. She got excited when I would do well, and somehow she made me believe I was going to conquer the world. After all those years of special classes and programs, not to mention all the homeschooling, I was finally beginning to improve.

Things started to click in my brain. I went from a 2nd grade reading level to a 7th grade reading level that year. I was chosen to be in the patrol (elementary school version of police) and I was able to go on the patrol trip to Washington, DC, as my older brothers did before me. My grades soared and everything was going my way.

I remember the first time I was reading and could actually visualize the images in my head. I freaked out. I worked so hard to put letters together up to that point that I had no idea you could see the images of what you were reading. It was better than a movie because it was mine, not someone else's. And in a move completely out of character for her, my mom caved. She allowed me go ahead and get my ears pierced, even though I received one C during the school year. She and my dad felt that I had done my very best, so in the summer between elementary school and high school, I joined the legions of teenaged girls with pierced ears.

Back when I was in school, our county didn't have middle school or Jr. High. We went straight from elementary school to high school. For some, it was a very difficult transition. But for me, it was my release from hell. I got to go to a new school, and no one there knew anything about my dyslexia. The kids from my old school knew my story, but what were the chances I would be in classes with them?

I was still in Special Ed, but there were only two of us in the class. So every day I would get one on one help from another teacher I adored, and I got to go to my regular classes with kids who had no idea that I had dyslexia.

Did I mention there were some really cute guys in my school? High School was a lot of fun. I joined the band and took up the clarinet, and I was horrible at it (you think learning to read words is difficult, try reading music), but I enjoyed it anyway. I went on to graduate on time, and I didn't become a teenage mother as was predicted earlier by the psychiatrist. Dispelling the rest of those predictions, I now drive everywhere, and I can read all the traffic signs.

Mama used her trail blazing voice to create and change the course of my life. She could have sat back and let the "system" handle me. Who knows, instead of being happily married with five incredible children, I could have wound up riding around on the city bus without the ability to find my way to the grocery store.

Instead, I helped raise some amazing children, and I am passionate about helping all children reach their full potential. I believe it is a God given right for children to be taught to read to the best of their abilities, and that no child should be denied access or passed over because they learn differently than other children.

Even now, when I come across an unfamiliar word, I can hear my mom say: "Calm down Laura. Sound it out." I don't know too many trail blazers. Most folks won't stand up for what they believe. Sometimes we are pushed by desperation, but my Mama is a trail blazer. And she did stand up for what she believed in, and she believed in me. Thank you Mama!

Alneata C. Kemp

The statement "Life after Death" has new meaning for me now. At one time I equated it to the scripture's reference of eternal life, but now it carries practical application for my day-to-day living. I'm Alneata C. Kemp, founder of the non-profit organization, Socks for Courtney.

Socks for Courtney was founded after the death of my nine year-old daughter, Courtney A. Kemp. Courtney died from undiagnosed heart disease. The day my husband, my two beautiful daughters, and I buried her, you might just have well placed me in the ground, for I too died that day. My best efforts could not yield a desire to carry on. That was until the Lord sent me my precious bag of socks. It was His and Courtney's way of reminding me to LIVE! From a simple bag of socks found in Courtney's room, new life began for me. My story is one of grief to greatness, and my mission is to continue to grace stages here in the USA and abroad to bring awareness for children with heart disease and to provide services worldwide to those in need.

To learn more about Alneata C. Kemp and Socks For Courtney, please visit us online at www.socksforcourtney.org, on facebook at: https://www.facebook.com/SOCKSforCourtney or by following us on Instagram and twitter at Socks for Courtney.

Alneata's Voice

From Grief to Greatness

Alneata C. Kemp

It wasn't supposed to happen this way. Parents should not have to bury their children, but this had become my horrible reality. It all happened incredibly fast. One day, we were preparing for her first day of school as a fifth-grade student, and the next day, we were preparing for her transition from earth to glory. The day I buried my child, I buried a piece of myself.

She had spent the summer with her grandparents, and on one occasion they mentioned that Courtney was awakened during the night because of a stomach ache and vomiting. We attributed this upset to many hours of riding her bike in the heat of the day, eating lots of junk food, and doing what she loved most, which was playing outside. She loved summertime fun at her grandparents!

She was ready for the first day of school on August 1, 2012. She was excited about seeing her friends, meeting new ones, and making lasting memories with her teachers. She even told her baby sister, Lauren, that she "could hardly sleep the night before" from the excitement and anticipation of the first day of school. She loved dressing up, and had decided to wear her blue jeans with her red shirt that day. She loved that shirt, mainly because it had an attached necklace.

It wasn't until the week of August 6, 2012, that Courtney started to complain to us of a headache. During the day, she would be okay, but at night this horrible headache would awaken her from her sleep. I started to sleep as light as a feather during this time, and the moment I heard her wake up, I ran down the hall to check on her. I can remember putting a warm cloth on her head just as I had done when she was a toddler. Somehow, the warm cloth soothed the pain, and when morning came she seemed to be just fine, and wanted to go to school. Regardless of how she may have felt, she wore the prettiest smile. She never lost herself through the pain that she experienced.

It was only a few days later, when I was helping Courtney with a homework assignment, that I literally saw her heart beat through her shirt. It happened so quickly that I thought that I was seeing things, but it was enough of a reason for us to race her to the ER. Once there, the doctor on duty examined Courtney, and decided to run several blood tests. He concluded that there were no signs of an infection of any kind, and that her blood work was great. He even went on to say that her heart was beating in tune for a healthy nine-year-old girl. Courtney sat on that table with the biggest smile ever. That was just the news we wanted to hear. We wanted to know from professionals in the field that she was okay.

Before leaving the ER we were told that if Courtney continued to complain of a headache, or if her symptoms worsened, we were to follow up with our Primary Care Physician. Well, the symptoms got worse. I can remember frantically calling the office of our Primary Care Physician because now, not only was Courtney complaining of a headache and vomiting; she was starting to lose her appetite. My phone message to them was that I felt like my baby was wasting away and that she had to be seen that day. An appointment was set and we felt relieved.

As we sat in the doctor's office, right before Courtney was seen, we talked about what she wanted for her birthday. She told me that she couldn't think of one thing she wanted, and she quickly changed the story and started to talk about the pretty green paint on the wall. She said, "When I get a house of my own one of my rooms will be this pretty green color." Her comment gave me hope, although I was thrown off guard by the fact that she didn't want anything for her birthday. I now believe that somehow she knew that she would be looking down on us from above when her next birthday came around.

The doctor stepped into the room, and there was silence from Courtney. She was timid and shy, but she had a way of getting her point across. We shared what was going on with her and, luckily, the doctor was able to pull the reports from our ER visit. She began to explain in great detail the results of her blood work. I remember it as if it were yesterday. I felt so comforted and hopeful that Courtney would be her old self soon. We were told that at Courtney's tender age of nine years old, it was likely that her body was changing. The doctor's final recommendation to us was to keep a diet diary, because she thought that maybe Courtney's body was having an allergic reaction to something she had eaten. We also had to give Courtney a baby aspirin to help with the headaches. She scheduled a date for us to have a CT scan done, saying she wanted to make sure that the headaches were not caused by something more serious.

Again, we were excited…they could not find anything physically wrong with our baby, and they suggested it was probably due to normal bodily changes that all girls will experience at different times in their lives. The few days leading up to our appointment for the CT scan resulted in many sleepless nights. Courtney's symptoms did not get worse but they didn't get better. I was holding on to the reports and diagnosis of the doctor. Today, I still ask myself why I trusted the doctors so much.

Courtney's CT scan was scheduled for August 17, 2012. We received a call from school that same day, stating that she had vomited while at PE. From August 1, 2012 to August 17, 2012, she had not missed any days of school. She left early a few times, but going to school was what she wanted to do. Her daddy picked her up from school and I met him at the hospital for her scheduled CT scan. She was not feeling well. I could see it in her eyes. She was so calm and relaxed on this day. We met the nicest nurse there who made Courtney feel so much better during the test. She was so patient, even as Courtney vomited on the table. She told us that it happens often because many people hate the idea of going into the tube for the scan.

The scan was done, and I asked Courtney what she would like to do next. She said, "Mom, I would love to have a salad." *"Oh, her appetite is coming back…she's feeling better,"* I thought. I was exploding with excitement, and took her to a local restaurant to get her salad. She took one bite of it and said, "I'm sorry you spent your money for that, Mommy." She was truly a little girl with a huge heart. She was always concerned about the feelings of others. I assured her that it was okay. In the meantime, I was glued to my phone, waiting on the results of the CT scan. I told her that if we didn't get a response from them before a certain time, then we were going to a different hospital in a different city. Minutes later the nurse called us to tell us that they had received the results of the CT scan and that everything looked great. She encouraged us to enjoy our weekend.

Again, the burden was lifted. I was reassured and was optimistic that Courtney would start feeling better soon. Previously, she had asked me "Mom, how is heaven?" I went into great detail about how wonderful heaven is, as I imagined it to be. I couldn't accurately put it into words, but I sure gave it my best shot. I remember how she sat next to me, looking directly into my eyes, as if she could see the excitement in my soul, merely by asking such a profound question. I wanted to paint a picture of heaven in her mind in the hope that it would be a story that she would always remember, and pass on to her children.

On Saturday, August 18, 2012, Courtney was up early. She was taking a shower. The door was cracked and I could hear her singing *Precious Lord Take My Hand*. When I heard her singing this song, it felt like she was singing with such conviction, and her request seemed so raw and real. Her grandparents visited and, although she said she was tired, she wanted to go to Wal-Mart with them. At this point, I was willing to let her do whatever she desired, as long as it made her feel better.

It was midnight and I heard her get up. I jumped up and raced to the bathroom where I found Courtney leaning over the toilet. I was so afraid, but I knew this wasn't the time to lose control. I told her, "Get up baby; come on baby, mommy is going to take you to the hospital." I called my husband, who was working an overnight shift, and told him that I was taking Courtney to the hospital. I was torn between calling 911 or taking her to the hospital myself. I felt that I didn't have a moment to lose. I told

Tyanna and Lauren to get up and go with me. They were as scared as I was. Secretly, I was encouraging myself while still trying to encourage all three of my girls.

I grabbed Courtney in my arms just as I did when I rocked her to sleep as a baby. I could hear her calling for me in a faint voice, "Mommy, mommy, mommy…" just as she would when she was three years old and wanted my immediate attention. We all were screaming her name, "COURTNEY". We were horrified, but she answered in the sweetest voice, as if our screams were disturbing her sleep. She was so tired. I raced to the hospital, flashing my headlights and emergency blinkers. I parked at the front entrance of the emergency room and ran in with Courtney in my arms. Her dad soon arrived and cuddled her in his arms until we were called to the receiving area.

They checked her over, reviewed her blood work, and tried to convince us, yet again, that everything was okay. At this point, Courtney was wearing that beautiful smile again. I refused to hear them; I refused to accept their assurance Courtney was healthy. I told them to scan her entire body, because something was wrong with our baby, and we were not leaving until it was done. After the scan, a doctor came in the room and told us that Courtney had pneumonia. We cried in relief. Finally, a true diagnosis!

I sent a message to our family and friends letting them know that Courtney was going to be okay. The doctor later came to us to report that our baby's heart was enlarged, and that they were transporting her to a Children's Hospital that was equipped to take better care of her.

The waiting seemed to last forever. I had no trust in the hospital, where we were going, but help was on the way. The ambulance ride, oh the ambulance ride was the longest ride of my life. I wanted to protect Courtney the way any parent would. I have never prayed so hard in my life. I told myself time and time again that everything was going to be okay. I reminded myself of scriptures that I had frequently shared with family and friends as they experienced various issues in their lives, and I remembered what I had preached to congregations big and small.

The scriptures were not speaking to me during this time and, honestly, I am not sure that I wanted to hear what they had to say.

I could see my baby kicking and pulling, just as she did when I carried her for nine long months. She was pulling for air and life, until finally, there was none left. At this point, we were diverted to the nearest hospital. As her mom, I realized that, for the first time, I was losing control. I couldn't decide the fate of her life, and there was nothing I could do to change that. We were called in a room where my baby laid lifeless on a barren wooden table. Courtney was gone. An autopsy revealed that Courtney's cause of death was Dilated Cardiomyopathy, a disease that enlarges the heart and causes it to fail.

I became numb after she passed away on that chilly Sunday evening of August 19, 2012. Although I had two other beautiful children, a wonderful husband, family members who would not leave our side, and a host of friends who prayed for us without end, I still could not imagine living without my daughter.

It wasn't until after her passing that I was reminded of various occurrences in her life. These incidents gave me the strength I needed to get up and live my life. Courtney was not an "A" student, but she was referred to as a "solid" student. The fact that she had to put in extra time and effort to learn her work didn't matter to her at all. She was up for the challenge, and learning and growing were what she enjoyed most.

The Lord has used Courtney's love of nature to nurture me back to his holy arms like never before. Her voice is not as loud as it once was, but the memories allow me to hear her whispers, and that has changed my life forever. I had to force myself to get up out of the horrible pit of grief, and allow the Spirit of the true and living God to place me within my purpose, so that I may live, grow, and properly belong.

As I remove weeds from my garden in preparation to plant new seeds, I hear the whisper of my sweet girl saying, *"Mom, find time to plant seeds and expect a bountiful harvest."* When the birds are flying over our home every morning, I hear the whisper of my sweet girl saying, *"Mom, today belongs to you. Take it by force and create everlasting memories."* When a bird stops by to have lunch from the menu that I created, I hear the whisper of my nature girl saying, *"Mom, a table shall be prepared for you to continue to feed all those who hunger."* When a butterfly comes to rest at my feet, I hear the whisper of my daughter saying, *"Enjoy the beautiful colors mom, because they will soon fade away."*

She is no longer here with us on earth, but I believe her purpose was so huge and so great that it could not be fulfilled completely on earth. Now, the spirit of Courtney is leading us and guiding us to places we thought we would never visit. Her whisper encourages me to embrace the small things of life, and to appreciate every moment that passes by.

At the time, it seemed easier to just run and hide but, thankfully, the whisper of God's beautiful little angel would not allow this to happen to me. Although it has taken some time to pull myself up, I AM up and I am here to stay.

This journey of grief and pain has not been an easy one. I would be lying to myself, and all of you, if I pretended it was anything but a dark journey of wrenching grief. But, for the past three years, each day has presented new challenges and awesome opportunities.

After Courtney passed away, we knew that, in order to create a new life, we would need professional assistance. We started to attend Grief Counseling, and it has saved our lives. Our counselor explained to us that dealing with grief is like standing in an ocean with our backs against the waves. He said, "We will recognize when a wave is coming; however, we will never know how big or small the wave may be." Some days, the wave may cover our heads and we may feel as if we are drowning in grief, but other days, the wave washes our feet and it is refreshing. The beauty is that no matter the size of the wave, by the grace of God we have been able to stand boldly to declare that the Lord has been with us through this dark journey.

Even today, Mill Creek Elementary School, Statesboro, Georgia, honors a deserving child each term. One who exemplifies truth, courage, and determination, with the Courtney Kemp award, in remembrance of Courtney. They vowed, "Once a Mustang, always a Mustang!" and they have kept their valuable word. As a family, we are dedicated to keeping the memories of our sweet girl alive (visit us at socksforCourtney.org), and we are committed to heart health education and public service.

With a heart of gratitude and a weeping soul of appreciation, I humbly shout THANK YOU to the heavens in the hope that my daughter hears me and knows that she was the biggest part of my life's transformation. I have been presented with the necessary tools to open my life's treasure box. This never would have been the case had I not buried my daughter, along with pieces of myself.

Someday, the whisper of the child that changed my life will be a whisper no more. Instead, I will hear a scream of celebration and "the voice that changed my life" and saved my soul will guide me into the heavenly courts. I'm now living this life on purpose, just to live again. And as long as I live...so shall our precious girl, Courtney Adavia Kemp.

Kim M. Martin

Life Empowerment Coach/Author/Speaker
Blog Talk Radio Co-Host

A Queens, New York native and Atlanta transplant, Coach Kim M. Martin, is a passionate speaker and storyteller.

Kim is the Co-Founder of Unlimited Love and Life Coaching, LLC where she shares her own testimony of tragedy and transformation; from filing for divorce {for the third time} to losing her 16-year-old daughter to a brain aneurysm.

Kim now inspires and empowers women from all walks of life to get {and stay} motivated as they "re-deFIND" themselves in pursuit of their passion and purpose.

Kim currently shares her motivational messages through the first book in her "From the Sideline" series entitled, "30 Days of Inspiration, From the Sideline..."

Kim is taking on her newest role as co-host of the blog talk radio show, Love Unlimited: Relationship Coaching with Kim and Sheronda. The ladies take a holistic approach to love and relationships on their weekly show which features live guests and listener call-ins.

Having obtained her Bachelor's degree in Business Management and an MBA in Human Resources, she is now pursuing her Doctorate of Business Administration in Industrial Organizational Psychology at Northcentral University.

You can find out more about Kim's coaching services and products at www.unlimitedloveandlife.com or email her at unlimitedloveandlife@gmail.com

Kim's Voice

The Loudest Voices Are Sometimes The Quietest Ones

Kim M. Martin

The voices that changed everything for me were the voices of my parents. No matter the time or distance, they are, and continue to be, the voices I hear under God's leadership. This has been put to the test in times of grief, and times of joy. Have you ever heard of a late term surprise pregnancy? Has the blight of crack cocaine ever touched your life? Has your world ever been rocked by unimaginable grief? No one could survive such trials without the rock solid support of a loving family. My parents' support and guidance as I sojourned through these experiences created the fearless woman that I am today. They have made it possible for me to run without abandon and to know that I am not only their child, but God's child.

Sometimes the loudest voices are the quietest ones. Sometimes they are the quietest because we need to listen to them more intently. Collectively, my parents were that quiet, small voice. The more closely I listened, the clearer their voices became.

My parents' voices were the clearest when I was in my last year of high school. I had been spending a lot of time "hanging out" at my house with a male friend of mine, whom I had known since I was 11 years old. My parents really liked him. He would go on early morning runs with my dad, and he was a regular at our dinner table. He attended almost all of our family functions.

When I was 17 years old, my family and I were attending a barbecue at my grandmother's house. My aunt (who was a nurse) pulled me and my mother aside to tell us that she believed I was pregnant! My mother and I looked at her in disbelief. My mother told her that she and I passed each other every morning coming out of the shower. She said it was impossible for her not to notice that I was pregnant. My aunt told my mother to look at my nose. We both smirked. If anybody knows *anything* about the Martin family, they know that we all have big noses! That didn't mean anything. My aunt suggested that I go to my gynecologist, just to be sure. My mother agreed and made an appointment for me the following week. We were both confident that there was nothing to worry about. My boyfriend, who by this time had become my fiancé, came along.

While I lay on the table waiting for the doctor to come in to conduct his examination, there was movement in my stomach that startled both my mother and I. It appeared to be a body part that went from one side of my stomach to the other. My heart sank. All I could think to myself was, "Oh my God! How could I not know I was pregnant? Weren't there supposed to be signs? Why am I feeling something for the first time NOW?" My aunt's diagnosis had been right. Upon further examination by the doctor, we discovered that I was eight and a half months into my pregnancy! I honestly had no idea. I had heard women speak about this happening, but didn't believe it was possible. I had begun taking birth control six months prior to this, and I could not believe I was one of the one percent of women who still get pregnant despite taking "the pill". I thought I was being responsible. I thought I had done the right thing by going to my mother and talking to her about having sex.

As the reality of what was happening began to hit me, the tears rolled down my face. This was not supposed to happen. I was supposed to start college in four months. How was I going to do that and take care of a baby too? My fiancé was allowed to come in the room and the doctor told him that we were expecting our first child. He was stunned, then came over and embraced me. Although this was not our plan, he let me know that he loved me, he still wanted to marry me, and that he would be right there when our baby was born. I was glad to know that he would be there for me, but my insides were still screaming, "How can this be?" All I could think about was what I was going to do with a new baby, and how I was going to prepare for motherhood in only two weeks!

My mother was calm and collected as we received the news. She let my fiancé and I know that we would figure out what we needed to do...and quickly! If she was disappointed with me, she did not show it. Her reaction to the news actually put me a little at ease, even though I felt as though my whole life had just flashed before my eyes. My mother suggested that we all go to my father's workplace and tell him about my pregnancy. I knew that my father would be disappointed. He had been looking forward to me starting college in the Fall. I also knew that even with my mother's support, I simply could not face my father with this news. I asked if she would talk to him first so I could take some time to compose myself. I was still in shock, and honestly didn't think I could say the words, "I'm pregnant" to him. My mother didn't object. She squeezed my hand and went in to talk to my father.

When she returned, she told me that my father was surprised, and that he just leaned up against the wall once she delivered the news. He couldn't understand how I was going to be able to start college and raise a child. A fresh set of tears began to fall. The thought of the expression on his face broke my heart. I was upset, but my mom assured me that everything was going to be okay. She let me know that we were going to get through this together. For the first time in my life, I felt like I had failed my parents. That feeling would weigh heavily on me until my daughter was born.

Kristine was a beautiful baby. She had the most perfect face I had ever seen. I spent countless hours just looking at her. Her father was right by our side, as promised. He would arrive at my house early and would not leave until she was asleep, because he did not want to miss anything she did. She was our greatest joy. My parents were smitten with her. There wasn't a moment of the day when she wasn't in someone's arms. She had everyone's attention. When she was in my father's arms, she would coo and smile the most. He would sing to her and she loved it!

Despite my father's love for Kristine, he did not speak to me until three months after my daughter was born. My daily, "Good Morning, Daddy!" went unanswered. This crushed my spirit because I have always had such an incredible love for my father. His decision not to speak to me only validated how I felt about failing my parents. The pain was almost unbearable. It was never my intention to hurt them. I was their baby girl, and I was going to be the first of their children to go to college and earn a degree. Contrasting the silence of my father was the encouragement of my mother. She helped me learn how to care for Kristine and assured me daily that everything would be okay. She reminded me that this was still my home, and that I was not going to be put out on the street with their granddaughter. She assured me that we were loved. Although my father said nothing, he still showed his love for me through Kristine. That was good enough for now. But it still hurt. My parents were never rude toward my fiancé and still treated him as though he were family. They respected his willingness to take care of Kristine and me.

Determined not to cause any more disappointment to my parents, four months after Kristine was born, I started college. My grandmother lived close by and offered to care for Kristine while I worked during the day and took classes at night. I was blessed to have a strong support system through my family.

Unfortunately, my focus on work, school and Kristine left my fiancé feeling ignored and inadequate. He felt as though I would not have enough room in my heart to love him and our baby. He also felt that because I was in college and he was not, I was going to think he wasn't smart enough for me. He feared that I would leave him, so he broke off our engagement. I was stunned and heartbroken. I felt like the two men I loved the most no longer loved me. I didn't think I would be able to bear the pain I was feeling. I knew that I could not let Kristine feel that pain through me, so I tried to mask my anguish. My mother stood by me and encouraged me not to give up. She would not let me believe that I wasn't still her beautiful, smart baby girl and that I was anything but a wonderful mother to Kristine. She assured me that my father would come around, and that I should continue to have faith that he would.

I believe it was my dad's love for my Kristine that finally broke the wall of silence, and encouraged him to speak to me again. When he finally spoke, all I could do was hug him and weep uncontrollably. I felt like I finally had my daddy back! A few years later, I came to realize why my dad didn't speak to me. He was disappointed. He did not want to hurt me with negative words. He realized that if he misspoke, his words would do more damage than his silence. When he was finally able to find the words to help rebuild my broken spirit, he decided to use them. That spoke volumes, because I knew he was protecting me.

Both my dad and my mom helped me through what could have been a devastating situation. I could have been a statistic. I could have been just another unemployed, teenage mother receiving government assistance ("welfare", etc.). I could have given up on my dreams of going to college and becoming a teacher. But, because my parents empowered me with their words and actions, I had the strength to move forward. I continued my college courses and began my career in the school system as a Paraprofessional, one year after my daughter's birth.

The support and encouragement I received from my parents prompted me to provide the same for my daughter. I believe I was successful in doing this not only for my first daughter, but for my second daughter, who would be born four years later. Two years after having my first daughter, I met my youngest daughter's father. He was a Security Officer at the school where

I worked as a Paraprofessional. After dating for two years, we got married and my youngest daughter Kathleen (aka "Kitty") was born soon after. Life was good…or so I thought. Just when I felt that I had overcome being a teenage mother and had become a responsible wife and mother, I discovered a crack pipe in my husband's coat pocket. We had only been married 4 months. I feared for my daughters' safety as strange men began to frequent our home. I packed up my things, took my daughters and moved across town. I filed for divorce the next day. I did not tell my parents what had happened until after I moved and the papers were filed. I was ashamed because my marriage had failed, so soon after it started. I thought I had done it right by not living with my husband prior to getting married. I never realized that at night, when he said he was working late, he was actually smoking crack. Although surprised, my parents did not pass judgment. They simply asked if I was okay and if I needed anything. I assured them I was okay and they did not interfere with my decision. They allowed me to continue to be the responsible parent I was to my daughters. This was important, because it taught me to deal with situations on my own. It gave me strength.

I would not be so lucky in love in the years that followed. I would marry and divorce two more times. Although we are no longer married, my third husband and I still remain close friends. This was my longest marriage, and he was there, along with my parents, to help me through one of the most traumatic experiences of my life.

By 2009, Kristine was finishing her last semester of college. She earned her degree in Video Game Design and Development and was scheduled to move up to New York to pursue a career in gaming. Kitty was a few months into her junior year of high school. She was my academic star. She had aspirations of attending an Ivy League school and becoming a clinical psychologist. Kitty was active in several school activities and was well liked by her classmates. She was 6'1, so she definitely stood out in a crowd! Everyone referred to her as my "mini-me". She had an infectious smile and a loving spirit that drew people to her. Kitty was my angel...in more ways than one.

I had gone back to school to obtain my MBA in 2008. I was taking three day weekend intensive classes at the time, in order to finish my degree by May 2010. On October 11, 2009, I came home from school expecting to be greeted by my husband and daughters. I had spoken to my husband and Kristine, but Kitty did not come out of her room to greet me as usual. She had been up late the night before, taking her braids out of her hair. Around 1 AM, I recalled telling her not to stay up too much longer. She could finish her hair in the morning. I gave her a kiss, told her I loved her and went to bed. When she didn't come out to greet me, I assumed she was sleeping. I finally went to her room to wake her up. She was lying on the floor. I didn't find this unusual, because she liked sleeping on the floor. As I went to rouse her from her sleep, I immediately realized that she was not snoring as she always did. Then I realized that she was not breathing. I called out to my husband to call 911. I turned my daughter over and began to perform CPR, but it was too late. She was gone. The last breath in my daughter's body was mine.

The coroner determined that Kitty had passed in her sleep several hours earlier. It took a month before his report came back with the cause of death. She had a brain aneurysm. The coroner explained that she had the type of aneurysm that manifested itself between the ages of 15 and 20. During that time, the blood vessels either burst, and the person suffered from a severe stroke and was left in a vegetative state, or they die instantly. There were no symptoms or warning signs. There was nothing preventive that could have been done.

My whole world stopped. I never thought in a million years that I would have to bury my own child. She was supposed to bury me. I know that the God I serve does not make mistakes. I am at peace with that. That still did not stop the pain of missing her. Once again, my parents were there to support me as I grieved for Kitty. Their voices comforted me as I gave Kitty back to God. It was the hardest thing I have ever done. My parents were there to support me as they had been countless times during the course of my life. It's what lifted me up and allowed me to move forward.

My parents were there for birth of my oldest child, and now for the death of my youngest. Everything my parents ever taught me about strength, love, responsibility and family all converged on me at one time. My faith in God made it possible for me to come to terms with Kitty's death and to get back to living my life. What I didn't realize was that He was not finished with me yet. Let me show you how God works. Almost one year, one month and one day after my daughter's death, my oldest brother passed away. God allowed me to support my parents in the way that they supported me. Their lessons came full circle.

My parents will always be the voice that whispers in my ear when I'm going through the ups and downs of life. They have consistently supported me in anything I have sought to do. Anytime I fall, they are there to pick me up and encourage me to keep running.

Over the last few years, I have learned the value of following my destiny. I am now a Certified Life Coach, Professional Speaker and an Author. I empower and inspire women to "re-define" themselves by living their authentic lives. It was what I was born to do.

For this, I honor John and Marie Martin as the voices that changed My Everything!

Elena Bazaldua

Maria "Elena" Bazaldua has been an inspiration to many, especially young adults. She has courageously paved a pathway for many to follow. She made up her mind to take the road less traveled even before she realized that it was indeed what she was doing. Her vision and passion for helping others achieve success is heartfelt and uplifting. Throughout her career as a secondary teacher, she has been able to connect with students, colleagues, and parents alike. In this chapter, Elena recounts the days of her childhood experience as a determined first-generation young girl on the quest for answers. Both her parents were born and raised in San Luis Potosí, Mexico. They immigrated to the United States in the mid 1970's and settled in Southern California. It was there where it all began for Elena.

In her junior year of college a seed was planted in her, which led to the beginning of her new journey in the world of network marketing. This part of her life has been most exciting. It has opened doors to endless possibilities not only in her career but has helped her profoundly master the art of relationship building. With her passionate and charismatic personality, Elena hopes to inspire the masses through her relatable story one chapter at a time. This is only the beginning of her journey as a writer. Her vision is extraordinary. The strength and transparency of Maria Elena Bazaldua is enlightening.

To contact Elena go to www.elenab.juiceplus.com or email: ebazaldua@gmail.com

A Time for Change

Elena Bazaldua

It was just another assignment from my teacher. No big deal, right? But that day, that teacher, that assignment, and the San Diego Padres changed my future. You don't always have the chance to pinpoint the moment your life changed, but I am one of the fortunate ones. Someone believed in me. And I want to tell you why that matters.

This chapter is dedicated to two very special ladies. These ladies have no idea that I am writing about them, and at the same time, *to* them. Thank you for being the voices that helped change my path, and helped me to find greatness in myself. The voices that spoke to me came from two teachers who went above and beyond to be there for me when I needed someone the most. My heart is overjoyed with gratitude!

My story began when I walked into Mrs. Humphrey's room without my homework. It was unusual for me not to do my homework. I didn't think one assignment would make a difference. Well, I was wrong! It was a big deal! Mrs. Humphrey was disappointed that day, I will never forget her reaction. Not one single student had done their homework that day. She looked at me with a sigh of anticipation and asked, "Elena, you have your homework, right?" Staring down at the floor, I softly said "no." Her face frowned, and we all received quite a lecture from her. I felt her disappointment in my heart! I knew she really cared, not just about me, but about all of her students! At the end of her lecture, she asked a few of us to come in during lunch to complete the assignment. I did. *That assignment changed my life.*

The Assignment

What was so important about a homework assignment? This was not just *any* homework assignment. This was a scholarship questionnaire from the San Diego Padres Baseball Team. In 1995 the team partnered up with the AVID program and awarded 25 students from San Diego County a $5,000 scholarship. I had no idea what "scholarship" meant. The only reason I went to finish the questionnaire during lunch was to make Mrs. Humphrey happy. I did not want to be a disappointment to her. I rushed through the questions, but I do remember being very honest with my answers. One question they asked was about sports. What was my favorite sport? I didn't have one. I was still not interested in baseball, even if the scholarship was a gift from the Padres. My father was very "machista" and believed sports were for boys, not girls. So I didn't stand a chance!

After reviewing the questionnaires by the San Diego County Office of Education, a couple of students from each participating school were selected to go in for an essay write up and a live interview. To my surprise I was selected! I still was clueless what this all meant, but it was good for a field trip away from my hometown! Mrs. Humphrey and Mrs. Craig took turns driving me to dinners, games, and ceremonies. This was a big deal! Yet neither of my parents realized the importance of this opportunity.

AVID, Mrs. Humphrey and Mrs. Craig would forever change the course of my life. What is AVID? AVID is an acronym that stands for Advanced Via Individual Determination. This was a program designed to help students prepare for college at a very early age. It is an outstanding program and, of course, with no hesitation, I agreed to be in AVID when offered the opportunity.

My Family

Up until middle school, I had struggled in school. I was born in San Diego, CA, but I moved to Mexico when I was a baby for a few years where my grandparents raised me. My parents immigrated to the United States in search of a better future, leaving the children behind until they were settled and financially capable of supporting them. Their education was very limited. In 1989 the family reunited in the Southern part of California. During these early years in our new home, school was not a priority; and English was a foreign language to us all! By the time I reached the seventh grade, I was fluent in English and wanted to learn all there was to learn. I remember having to work twice as hard as some of my classmates, and I stayed up late doing homework regardless of the circumstances at home. I wanted to do well in school. And most of all, I wanted to please my teachers.

México

My parents married in their teen years. They were very young, and started a family right away. My father was egocentric and controlling. My mother was submissive and practiced what she had learned her entire life, which was to follow her husband.

"Good or bad till death do us part," were my grandmother's words of advice to her. I was a child, and I didn't understand the pain my mother was in, and the turmoil it would cause in the future. All I knew was the void I felt in my soul. I missed my parents. I yearned to be with them and my siblings felt no different. A few months before my youngest sister turned one, my father sent for my mother, again. He thought it would be a good idea that she went alone and left all four kids with her mother. My grandma had a beautiful soul, but she was tired and overworked. She lived in a beautiful village in the mountains of San Luis Potosi, Mexico.

Life in "the rancho" was simple. Children went to school only if the teachers showed up! It was a long trip for the teachers to make up the mountain every day. Rainy days were the worst. They never showed up. But when they did, it was a great day! Families demonstrated their gratitude by cooking hot meals for them. The teachers were highly esteemed by the families. Often times it was my grandmother who gladly opened the doors to her house.

The day my mother had to depart came unexpectedly. She didn't want to leave any of her children, but she had to. This time she left my two sisters, one of whom was a baby and my eldest sister of seven years old.

Mid 1980's in America

For the first time my mother had gone against my father's will and took two kids with her to the United States, my brother and me. We were four and five years of age. It was a hard decision for my mother, I know. No mother in her right mind wants to leave her baby or any of her children thousands of miles away!! Yet, my father didn't see it this way. And this was not the first time my mother was up against the wall. She was helpless.

Two years went by and my little brother and I had experienced and seen way too much domestic violence in the home. The scars were as deep as those of my sisters who had been left behind. My father was abusive, a cheater and cold hearted. Just a few months after my new youngest brother was born, my mother headed to Mexico with her three kids at hand to reunite with her daughters. For the first time in two and a half years, we were all together! My mother had found the courage to go against my father and follow her heart. Her children were her whole world and she was ours. The trip to Mexico combined joy and heartbreak. My little sister knew her grandma "abuelita Cuca" as her "mama," which left her biological mother seeming like a stranger. There was joy that mother and children were reunited and that we would all be going back to the U.S with her. But at the same time the heartache was unbearable for my sisters, mother and grandmother.

The family's adjustment to life in the USA was difficult. Our small two bedroom apartment only got smaller as the years went by. Nevertheless, we were happy to be together, as it should have been all along. Finding a quiet space to do homework or read a book wasn't always possible. Wait, we did not own books! Both of my parents worked full time to support the family. It was clear that we had to attend school, but neither parent knew how to support us in our studies. The fast growing town of Escondido, which is located North of San Diego, was still very foreign to them, yet here we were living in the middle of a gang neighborhood, and in a house full of drama. I wanted to escape, to go far away, and never look back. There was no escape.

The fights at home kept getting louder and louder. I could not understand why my mother continued to cook, clean, wash, and wake up at four in the morning to prepare lunch for a man who barely even noticed her. Why would my mother put up with that kind of treatment? Did he not love her? Or us? Was this the way marriage was supposed to be? I had so many questions.

We all needed an outlet, and we were going to find love and acceptance "somewhere." My oldest sister had a huge responsibility to help take care of the youngest siblings and tend to the house. My brother had no relationship with my father. He was the scapegoat of the family. He was always looking for a place to go. It wasn't long before he was part of the local gang. Before we knew it, he was in juvenile hall; and once again, our family was separated. My father thought beating him would make him stop hanging out in the streets; instead he pushed him further away. No one was equipped to help my brother, as he was young and weak and the adults were lost and hurting.

My brother has spent most of his life in prison. He is currently out of prison and living with my mother. Once again, we are doing all that we can to support him and help him get his life in order. He has work to do! Yes, he does! He needs to do his part as well. We are all hoping for the best.

Looking back now, each one of my brothers and sisters were affected in a different way by the choices made by our parents. How many times do we come across a person who has overcome adversity? Not often enough. I feel very fortunate to have had loving and caring people that listened to my cry for help.

Perseverance overcame my struggles. Today is a new day, and I am no longer confused. I no longer hide my pain with a smile. Today I am healed. Today I do not feel like escaping. Today is a great day to say, "Thank you." That scholarship was indeed my ticket to venture out into the world, where the possibilities of becoming "great" are endless. Today I look back to this era of my life and realize that this time in my life was crucial! And I can never repay these amazing ladies for their kindness.

I was able to stay afloat and complete all of the requirements to apply to four-year colleges. I was accepted at three out of the four. I chose to attend the one furthest away from home! I am glad I did. The scholarship was the "hook" that kept me pushing through anything life had in store for me.

During my sophomore year in college, my parents finalized their divorce. After 25 years of marriage, the best was yet to come. I have been stubborn and have not always listened to what He is telling me. But surely, my Creator is loving and awesome. I have come a long way and am so excited for the next phase.

Mrs. Humphrey

Dear Mrs. Humphrey,

Thank you! Thank you! Thank you! I do not know if I ever thanked you enough for all that you did for me!!

"This is so bizarre," was one of your favorite phrases. I still remember your colorful matching Disney outfits! I mean really, who works at the Disney store during the summer? You! And I admire you for raising your daughters on your own after losing your husband and son in that fatal accident. It takes strength and dedication to carry on, and work with a population of kids who don't stand a chance because of demographics. Yet, you cared. Thank you for investing your time and helping me build my future. I didn't know that 20 years later, I would be filled with gratitude for the moments you shared with me. I remember with a smile the long drives, the

lunches, the tutoring, the college field trips, and the slumber party at your home!!! You are amazing, and I wish you nothing but the best during your retirement years from one of the most rewarding careers in existence.

Xoxo,
One lucky student

Mrs. Craig

Dear Mrs. Craig,

You are the "greatest" teacher in the world! I am so blessed to have had you in my life when I did. Your letters during high school and college, and now your Facebook messages, still touch my heart every time. Thank you for believing in me and for adding hours to your already long workdays. The years you invested in your career touched many lives. That is a fact. You are loved and appreciated. After teaching for eight years myself, I realize it takes heart to do this extraordinary job that many see as "ordinary." You made Language Arts fun! Your projects allowed me to step out of my comfort zone and be the best that I could be. And I am so glad I was able to share beautiful memories with you at the stadium. Life is good!

Xoxo,
Your #1 fan

Gratitude

I am grateful for having had two angels that embodied life to me. I stand proud of my journey and the people I have met along the way. I realize that without guidance during my pre-teen years, anything could have happened. What if I had decided not to complete that special AVID assignment during lunch? Where would I be now?

This brings me to today. Every decision I made in my life had a consequence. That is the nature of life, and we must learn from our mistakes. One of the greatest lessons in my life concerns accountability. Despite my childhood experiences and past mistakes, I woke up every day and had the opportunity to get up and try again.

I came to a crossroad in my life where I realized that I could not blame others for anything that was happening in my life! At this point, I had become a mother myself. When my son was born, so was I. Any day is a good day to be born again! When I held this little guy in my arms, I met unconditional love for the first time. I understood my mother and I cried for all that she had to endure. I was resentful towards my dad but realized that change happens from within. His time will come when he is ready. I still have hope for him. I realized when my son was born that if I wanted my life to change, I had to change. So I did.

Let me begin with the mindset. I know there is a source greater than I. I know in my heart that He makes no mistakes. A clear message of His unconditional love came to me a few years ago as I found myself broken, again. At that moment I surrendered my life to the Creator of my life. I began to spend time in meditation until I regained strength.

After my son was born, I struggled a lot with my relationship with his dad. The thought of being a single mother scared me but not as much as the thought of spending 25 years with a man who did not love me and respect me. Year after year I found myself starting all over! I was tired and worn out, and I was only in my twenties! Something had to change. I deserved better and so did my son. My only salvation was within me, in knowing that I was not alone. There was a light shining on me every hour of every day.

Through this process, many revelations came to me. It was very clear that my angels have always watched over me. I was awakened. I am meant for greatness and so are you. You just have to know that you know. There is always room for growth.

I am an educator at heart. I will soon begin my ninth year of teaching. I truly enjoy building relationships with my students. My goal has always been to pay it forward and make a difference by touching students' lives the way Mrs. Humphrey and Mrs. Craig touched mine. I know this is not a coincidence. Both of these beautiful ladies will forever be a part of my story. I am now in my early thirties and I am discovering a world full of possibilities. I have to stay true to my heart, and I will continue touching lives by helping others to develop their true potential. Just as Mrs. Craig believed in the GREAT person inside of me, I know each one of you reading this story also has the spirit of greatness inside your soul waiting to be unleashed!

As I give thanks for the influential voices in my life, I am closing a chapter and beginning a new one. I am embarking in my new journey as an entrepreneur. I will always resonate with the teacher spirit because it is what I have known my entire life. I have had amazing teachers and students!

Reflecting on my childhood experiences allows me to never forget where it all began. Many strong women have paved the way and will continue to do so. I am proud of my mother and how far she has come in her life thus far. I plan to chart a better course for my children and future generations to come. The legacy of "Elena the great" is just beginning to unfold.

Deborah Crowe

As the CEO of a successful medical case management practice for 23 years, Deb Crowe recognized the growing need for further support for professionals and families dealing with catastrophic illnesses.

Leading this new vision, Deborah has evolved into a Work Life Balance Specialist and has created a model for revitalization, stress management and leadership success.

Deborah Crowe is a natural born thought leader. Her clients have welcomed her mentoring style which includes high energy, a great sense of humour, a positive attitude and the ability to never see barriers, only opportunity. She brings out the best in

all of her clients with integrity and true authenticity.

Deborah supports men and women who have placed themselves on the backburner in life. She boosts them emotionally and gives them the tools to manage employment, family and self so that they can regain their Work Life Balance. It's not about strategy; it's about a new way of thinking.

Deborah brings a level of grit as an entrepreneur like no other. She is extremely resilient and has demonstrated this ability in her own life. Setting constant goals and being a lifelong learner is her daily mantra.

Contact Deborah:
Direct: (519) 878-5839
Website: www.mamadeb.com
Twitter: @MamaDebCrowe
Facebook: www.facebook.com/MamaDebsKitchen

Deborah's Voice

All You Need is Love

Deborah Crowe

They say that life is not about the number of breaths you take, but the moments that take your breath away.

She was one of the few people I know who truly had an amazing life. She was the voice that never failed to give us the comfort we needed as well as the best of advice. A woman of principle and courage, she always stood strongly for what she believed in, and it is from her that I have learned to stay strong.

She was more than that, however. She was also a woman with a gentle smile and a soothing voice. I remember too, how she would hum and sing the lines of a favorite song in a faltering voice while walking around the house or sitting on her couch. Often times I would walk in as she was chatting with my grandfather, who was alive in her heart, but no longer in this world. She would look at me and giggle, and I would pretend I didn't hear her.

There are so many other things I remember—like the way she loved pastel colors, how she loved to eat fish and chips, or enjoy a cup of hot tea—all those little things. And it is during these moments that I realize how in the end, what we remember best are not really the grand gestures, but all the tiny yet necessary bits of a person's character.

I'm afraid there's only so much that my voice and my emotions can handle as I remember her. I believe it would be enough to say that having her in my life was a true blessing. She taught me what it meant to be alive and to love. She filled a space in me that my parents never could.

It was 1968, I was two years old. I was standing in my wooden play pen in the living room of our house. Being a toddler and having such insight to know what was going on around me was absolutely thrilling. I was bright, alert and through my non-verbal communication and intuition I knew that what my blue eyes were seeing was not right. This early childhood experience secured a foundation in my soul that I deserved better. While having a photographic memory can be a blessing, those vivid childhood memories have been turned into lessons of gratitude and shaped me into who I am today, a middle-aged woman full of gratitude and amazing stories of how my level of gratitude came to be.

I was born the youngest of five in 1966. I had three older brothers and one older sister. My mother used to tell me that my birth was not planned and that I was not like my older siblings. I knew from a young age that I was destined to be something great.

My father was an entrepreneur who was not home very often, and my mother was the model of a good housewife. She dressed nicely each day and the house was spotless. The children were always kept clean and quiet, and meals were always on time, especially dinner. We were to be seen and not heard when my father finally did arrive home.

Dinner was served to you (condiments and all). There was no choice. You ate dinner or you went to your room (I was very thin!) I learned from a young age to enjoy my own company, and the solitude of quiet.

We wanted for nothing as children. We had every materialistic thing that money could buy. We had a lovely, clean home, and took vacations every year. However, the maternal, loving mother you might expect in this scenario was not present. Her days consisted of her regular routine of cleaning, taking cigarette breaks, ensuring her kids were not dirty, more cleaning, and then finally, calling her girlfriends. At 3:00 p.m. the neighborhood wives' club congregated in our kitchen to watch their favorite soap opera and have cocktails and chain smoke, until it was finally time for them to go home and prepare dinner for their families.

My father was a busy entrepreneur and uprooted our family quite regularly. We did not live in any home for more than two years. I had just started kindergarten and was beginning to develop my social circle, but I never got very far. Once first grade started, I was already at a new school and living in the country on a farm. I was starting over, again.

The country was my safe ground, my favorite place. We had a dog, rabbits, horses, cattle, ducks and 100 acres of gorgeous farm land where I could roam, run, sing, dance and play. I spent the next two years at the farm and I loved it. My dog Reuben and I ran behind the barn, where I sang and gave concerts, and he acted as my attentive audience, with his wagging tail. I had a couple of friends and attended Brownies at the local church, but that was the extent of my social involvement.

The next year, at age 9, we moved again. This time it was back to the city, into a semi-detached home. I always treated every move as an adventure as I am very imaginative and my young mind thought I should view it as a positive. It was the best way to deal with it, as I had no choice in the matter. I loved my new L-shaped room, and my closet was the coolest. But after this move my life changed forever.

Each day when I arrived home, my mother maintained her cocktail hour. Now, however, she had to do it alone as she had yet to meet a new circle of friends. My mother was socially shy and perhaps inept, so she made no effort to find a new social circle. My siblings were older now and had their own lives and their independence, and my oldest brother was now married and starting his life with his new wife.

I was truly longing to have that close bond with my mother, full of maternal wisdom, affection and playfulness. It was only a dream for me. Then the voice that changed everything came to my rescue. It was my father's mother, Elizabeth Gertrude Martin. She was born in Liverpool, England on March 11, 1908. I truly idolized her from birth, but I remember her vividly from age two. English born with strong Irish roots, she was my true role model in life and she was like my second mother. We had a very special bond and she brought out of the best in me. She loved to be called Lil, and played a mean game of euchre (a card game). For 11 months of the year, if she drank, it had to be dark rum and coke. In December, however, it was dark rum and eggnog to celebrate the Christmas season.

One of the best life experiences she gave me was taking me to church. She created my love of faith in all aspects of my life and taught me that God is always with me, during the good times and bad. All I had to do was ask for his help, guidance and direction.

I was never alone. This was an epiphany for me as when I was home, I truly felt alone most of the time.

She possessed so many wonderful traits. She was intelligent and had an amazing sense of humor. But most importantly, she taught me to accept people with disabilities. When she was a young girl, she was diagnosed with polio in her right leg. The doctors in England wanted to amputate her leg but my great grandmother Alice would not allow it.

They decided instead to immigrate to Canada. They sailed across the Atlantic Ocean and moved to Toronto, Ontario, Canada. The doctors were able to save my Nana's leg, however, it was quite small (the size of a small wrist) and her foot was crooked and her toes had to be fused. This did not slow her down, and she used to joke about it! Her feet were different sizes so she hated shoe shopping! When she walked, she would lead with her left leg and the right leg/foot would drag/follow. This was not a disability to her. She demonstrated to me that she could do anything she wanted to do. She just put her mind to it and it would be done! She even nicknamed her 'bad' leg as her 'gammy leg'. We used to laugh so hard about this!

From the age of nine until well into my teen years, we spent every single weekend together. Nana picked me up and brought me to her house and I loved it! When I got home on Sunday night, I dumped my suitcase right into my hamper and repacked for the next Friday, and thought to myself, "five more sleeps then back to Nana's house." Every night I thanked God that she was in my life. She shaped and molded my character during my most challenging years.

Nana taught me core beliefs and values that are simple, yet necessary. She called it true common sense. If you treat people the way you like to be treated, you will never go wrong. I have never wavered from this core belief.

She enhanced my entrepreneurial skills as well. My older siblings got $1.00 a week in allowance from her. However, I persuaded her to consider inflation, and got my allowance raised to $2.00 per week! She used to laugh at me and shake her head!

Even though I had a biological mother, Nana truly felt like my real mother, in my eyes and affectionately in my heart. I still reminisce about our weekends, and all the beautiful memories we created together. She gave me a love of baking and cooking, and she gave me an appreciation of our cultural roots in England and Ireland. She used to travel to Ireland to see relatives, and I always loved the smell of her suitcase when she came home and opened it up. I could smell the ocean!

When she stopped driving, we walked everywhere or took the city bus. My fondest and favorite adventures were always on Sunday. As we walked to church, I skipped alongside her, chattering and carrying on, while she just smiled and hoped my energy would be used up before we got to the church! We played together and often had tea parties with freshly made baked goods. She showed me how to roll the homemade dough with her arthritic hands, while we chatted and sang or listened to her favorite music. Our favorite snack with our tea was her famous jam buddies!

The single best attribute that I possess today, one that I am so grateful for, is the voice I have because Nana taught me to speak up and be heard. She taught me to be who I am and not be fearful. She showered me with love and affection and told me I would do great things in my life.

My Nana's hearing declined as she aged, to the point that she wore two hearing aids. As I write this, the memories have me laughing out loud. Sitting in church, she would adjust the volume setting to hear the minister, and of course the choir! Both hearing aids were whistling away and her 'gammy leg' was tapping on the floor and she was having a grand old time. I had to elbow her (gently of course) and gesture for her to lower the volume, and she nodded to me.

Relocating so often was very difficult for me as a child because I never felt that I was able to settle in anywhere. The inconsistency of developing and sustaining friendships was hard as I never seemed to have enough time to be with my new friends. This made me feel that I did not have a sense of belonging, or even a foundation.

Nana's weekends assisted me in molding my character and making me who I am today. She instilled good, strong core beliefs and values, and a level of faith that grows daily. She listened attentively to my dreams and never judged. However, she would often have the inquisitive look of "how are you going to do that?"

In 1987, my dad passed away at 54 years old. Nana and I stayed at the hospital around the clock for almost a week that September. He passed away in the early hours on a Sunday. It was beyond heart wrenching. I was only 21 years old, and my Nana had lost her only child. Burying a child is something no parent ever wants to experience.

After my dad passed away, I felt lost and did not know which way to turn or where my life was headed. They say that time heals all wounds, and that cliché is so true. We kept his memory alive by chatting about him, telling stories and celebrating his life.

As a young adult, my life carried on. Nana celebrated my first new car with me and loaned me the money to buy it. It was a 1988 Pontiac Firefly. I adored this car! It was light grey, with four doors and a hatch back and sun roof! It even had a stereo and cassette player. This was a huge positive milestone in my life and once again she was there to share in this with me.

In 1990, I decided to start my own company. My dad's name was David William, so in his honor and to keep him and his entrepreneurial spirit alive, I created the name Davwill Consulting Inc. and my company was born!

I was now working with many new contract clients and living in my own apartment, and my life was taking shape. It was 1992. Nana was living with my sister Jo-Anne in Port Dover, Ontario, Canada. It was a 90 minute drive from where I was living. We talked on the phone and wrote letters, and I saw her every couple of months.

Since 1990, I had been dating a man named John Crowe. Nana was very fond of him and in 1991 he asked me to marry him. It was with excitement that I went to visit Nana and show her my engagement ring. She was so excited, and we discussed the wedding plans, and set the date, September 18, 1993. I envisioned her sitting in the front pew of the church during my wedding, and could not wait for that moment.

In December 1992, my mother, older brother and his family decided to go visit Nana. I wanted to go with them, but the weather was not great that day and we were expecting a lot more snow, so I was unable to go. It was only four days later when Nana passed away. My heart was truly broken that day, December 17, 1992. My best friend, confidant, substitute mother and wing partner had gone to be with the Lord. I was overwhelmed with sadness to the point that I felt sick. I deeply regret that I did not get to see her, hug her, or say goodbye.

There is always a funny story with Nana, even with her passing. She always told me she was going to pass away in her sleep. She was true to her word. She was so innately organized that she had all her affairs in order. She had a bed that she adjusted to prop her up comfortably so she could watch television in her bedroom. Her tea caddy was beside her as she watched the local evening news. My sister usually checked on her before she went to bed, however, on this night she did not. Nana had this all divinely crafted. She passed quietly in her sleep and my sister told me that when she went into her room, Nana looked very peaceful. She was 84 years old.

I went to my church and arranged to have a service of celebration for Nana and her amazing life, and I wrote and gave the eulogy. My priest was so comforting and supportive, and said he was honored to have me participate in the celebration. Nana was cremated, and we brought her ashes to the church and put her right up front for everyone to see! She always loved a good gathering. I wrote and gave one of the best speeches of my life. I was honoring a women who was always there for me, and had a significant impact on who I am today. Nana helped me develop as a person and appreciate life, one step at a time. Through laughter and tears, my eulogy conveyed what a rich, full life she had lived. She learned from her mistakes and most importantly, she always carried on. After the service we had a lovely luncheon at a restaurant, where we laughed, cried and reminisced with family and friends.

Keeping a loved one's memory alive is how, in my opinion, you honor them. To this day, when I am troubled, confused, curious, etc. I ask her for guidance or a sign. She conveniently complies by leaving a nickel coin for me to find. Every time I ask, a nickel appears. Then there are days when I am working in my home office and I can smell her perfume (Chanel No. 5) or her night cream (Oil of Olay) as if she's in the next room. I truly believe she is with me. I have a picture of her behind my desk on the bookshelf and another picture of her with her mother Alice, on her wedding day, in my home office.

I guess you can say that I've not let her out of my sight. She is with me daily and has made a lifelong impression on me. I am who I am today because of this amazing women, whom I was blessed to have had as my Nana. On my wedding day, I followed the tradition of something old, something new, something borrowed, something blue. Nana once gave me a beautiful handkerchief from Ireland that had embroidered blue flowers on it. I wrapped that handkerchief around the base of my flower bouquet, and held it close to me. She was there with me in spirit and holding my hand.

David Bossen

David Bossen graduated cum laude from the University of Georgia in 1980 with a degree in business. After a few years in the corporate world, he started his own business in the telecommunications field which he has been operating since 1986. In his spare time, he enjoys playing guitar, writing, geology and drawing. He also published a newsletter for a number of years. Married 27 years, he and his wife Darice have a daughter and reside in Kennesaw, GA.

His blog named Big Thumbs and Freedom can be found at www.writerwrongusa.blogspot.com.

David's Voice

Climb Every Mountain

David Bossen

T he voice that still speaks to me across the decades is not loud, audacious or even memorable. It came in a passing moment that, if not for the circumstances, would be long forgotten. At the time, I didn't even realize the lesson I was about to learn. And the person who spoke to me was not a mentor or authority figure. He was just a friend who had no idea of the importance of what he told me, or more accurately, shouted at me.

I attended the University of Georgia back in the 70's. The tone of the times was post-Viet-Nam, and the hazy feel good times of the 60's was morphing into the reality of earning a living. The catchphrase of the era, "If it feels good, do it" was exposed as idealistic psychobabble after it dawned on us that everything you have to do in life doesn't feel good, and some things that feel good have disastrous consequences.

How does an insecure college kid, launched from a broken family and drug infused peer group, manage to transition into a position of personal responsibility on a college campus? Well,

I can tell you that Schlitz Malt Liquor is not a good strategy. But as the semesters flew by, I found my groove and kept up my grades, and even found a wonderful girlfriend.

Still, I felt so insecure inside, and I worked to keep it hidden from everyone around me. I covered it up with Dean's list grades, nightclubs, and the fact that I had a girlfriend to hang out with. Looking back, I was really doing pretty well, even though it didn't feel that way at the time. So when my roommate and his friends asked if I wanted to join them on a climbing trip to the north Georgia Mountains, I accepted immediately, eager to add mountain climbing to my list of accomplishments. After all, who couldn't climb some rocks? (Yes, someone is going to eat their words soon.)

Our destination was Mount Yonah in the Appalachian foothills. It featured many exposed granite faces for climbing and rappelling. The Army Rangers sometimes used that location for training, adding to the machismo of the expedition. When we arrived, it was a perfect day, with clear blue skies and a light breeze.

Climbing involves a myriad of gear, including ropes, hooks, anchors and so forth. We trudged along with our gear clinking, and as a warm up, we decided to rappel off of a large boulder, where you walk backwards right off the edge, until you are hanging from the rope as you walk straight down the face of the rock. It reminded me of the old Batman show, where the caped crusader would often been seen walking down the side of a building in search of the bad guy.

After we all took turns, and pictures, it was time to move on to the more challenging climbing section. Here is where rock climbing etiquette comes into play. Many times a climber will dislodge some debris or drop some equipment during the ascent, and the protocol is to shout "Rock!" as loud as you can, so the climbers below will know to watch for falling rocks, or hooks, or anything else that could put a dent in someone's head.

As it turns out, that warning is not particularly helpful. The falling debris takes such an erratic path that there is little you can do besides pray. As we gathered at the base of a climbing wall, someone up high and out of view yelled "Rock" and we all looked up and braced ourselves. Sure enough, we could see a small rock bouncing haphazardly down the face of the cliff, headed toward our group. We all scattered, but there were few places to hide, so we all ran back and forth as the rock skipped from one direction to another. It may have been 5 seconds, but it felt much longer. Finally, the rock jumped sideways one last time and whizzed past my head with the combination of a whooshing and buzzing sound. We all laughed nervously and continued on our way.

Now I am getting to the point of this story, where a few words from my friend Mike Cole changed my outlook on life forever. Mike was an experienced climber, and treated me as his pet student, offering advice and tips about life on the rocks. We were a group of four climbers, all of us roommates in the same dorm.

We made our way to the base of another rock face, which looked to me to be almost vertical, with few handholds or footholds to choose from. Mike said this would be a good wall to climb, and told me to go ahead and give it a try. When climbing in this fashion, a couple of guys will take a safe route up to the top of the cliff and throw down a safety rope for the climber to attach to. They will then anchor the rope to a tree or boulder, and provide tension on the rope, so if the climber falls, they won't fall too far.

Once connected to the rope, I looked up, trying to find a pathway up this sheer rock face. I shouted up to Mike "I don't think I can climb this, there's nothing to hold onto!" He shouted back down "Go ahead and try. People climb this all the time. You can do it."

And there it was, my Voice! I admit it wasn't particularly notable or inspirational, and no music played from on high. But Mike told me that this wall could be climbed and that others had done it, so by God, I was not going to be embarrassed in front of my friends. I tightened the rope on my harness and yelled "Tension", which told Mike to yank the rope upward to take out the slack, and provide me with a bit of badly needed upward lift.

I gingerly made my way up the first section, carefully picking my handholds and trying to keep my feet on any solid bumps or rocks that could help me stay attached to that slice of granite. As the ground disappeared below me, I slowly made my way about halfway up the wall before I hit a section that simply offered no way to continue. I looked out over the valley, and down at the ground way below me, and decided I would have to go back down. I yelled up at Mike that I couldn't go on, and he yelled back "You can do it. Don't stop, just keep going. People climb this wall all the time."

I was scared, but I yelled back to keep a lot of tension on the rope, and that I would try to make it. I looked up at the sheer face above me, searching for anything I could grip. Here was a small notch, there was a tiny protrusion, but overall it looked hopeless.

"Tension!"

I decided that if I had no good handholds, I would flatten my body against the face of the rock and use the friction to prevent myself from sliding down. Then, I grasped at whatever small grips I could find and began to slowly inch my way up the face of the granite.

"Tension!"

At any moment I expected to slide off the rock and dangle in mid-air above the valley, protected only by a small rope attached to a small guy who had been drinking heavily the night before. My options were limited. There was no way to go back down without falling or being lowered back down by a sneering room-mate, and the way up was daunting. But, going up seemed to be my best option. I took a deep breath and shimmied my way up to another small ledge, then worked my way sideways to another outcrop, and basically crawled like a snail on a window up the remaining sheer face.

When I got to the top, Mike just looked at me and said "See, that wasn't so bad, was it?"

"Mike, that was the hardest thing I've ever done. Seriously, there wasn't anything to hold onto. I think you dragged me up that wall."

Mike just laughed. "Man, it's not that hard a climb." The Voice that Changed Everything, the magical inspiration in my life, was...sneering at me.

At this point, you might not think there was much of a lesson here, and you would be right. "Keep trying!" Who hasn't heard that before? But what happened next is the moment that changed my perspective on life. And it turned my simple climb into a life lesson. If you like delicious irony, you'll like what's next.

"Ok," I said. "You climb it!"

He immediately accepted. Of course he did. He had to show me how a real climber would make short work of this particular challenge. We switched places and he made his way back down to the base of the cliff. I grabbed the rope that was tied to the base of a tree and wound it around my waist, while bracing my feet against a large rock. Now I would be providing the tension, as my roommates looked on.

Mike yelled up to me that he was ready, and I tightened the rope. I was able to peer over the edge and see him adjusting his straps and preparing to climb. He took a few moments to assess the path, and started up the wall. I could judge his progress by how much rope I was taking in.

"Tension!" Yes, I expected to hear that shouted request. Then, a pause. A long pause. I looked over the edge. Mike was only a third of the way up the wall, staring up, scanning, searching. I said nothing. I knew what he was thinking. I felt the rope vibrate a bit as he jostled around, looking for a way to continue. Then another long pause.

"Hey, what's happening?" I yelled down.

"Give me a minute!" came the impatient reply.

Another minute went by, and I looked over the edge again to see what the holdup was. Mike yelled up at me "Slack, feed me some slack!" I loosened the rope and felt it slide through my fingers as Mike made his way back down to the ground. Confused, I tied up the rope and hurried back down to the bottom of the cliff.

"Mike, what happened?"

Mike was a quiet kind of person who rarely looked you in the eye when he spoke. He said nothing at first, then simply said "I couldn't do it. I don't know how you did it."

I was shocked, and pressed him. "What do you mean? You said other people climbed this cliff before."

"Maybe they have. I don't really know. Congratulations, you're the climber of the day." With that, he picked up his backpack and walked away, as our roommates came back down with the rope.

At the time, I was full of youthful pride. I had conquered that cliff as a novice, while my teacher had to turn back. And so the day continued, and we all had fun until we finally made our way back to campus that night. That day was soon forgotten and we all went on with our studies, our graduations and our lives.

Actually, I never forgot.

And this is the reason that day was so important in my life. When Mike told me I could make the climb because others had made it, I believed him. In my mind, it was possible, even though it didn't look that way from my vantage point. And because I believed it, I did it.

As it turns out, those words that inspired me to do the impossible were just trash talk from a guy who was trying to encourage me. He didn't really know if anyone had climbed that wall before; he just wanted to give me a challenge. But I didn't know that. I just knew it could be done, so I did it.

The importance of that lesson is still with me, and I will explain it here in simple language. If you believe you can achieve something, you will find a way to achieve it. If you doubt yourself, or listen to negative people, you are setting yourself up to fail. I was not a skilled climber, but somehow I found a way to accomplish a task that was later deemed to be impossible by my experienced friend. And can you imagine what went through Mike's mind? He saw me climb to the top (a good life metaphor, don't you think?) and so he had the advantage of knowing it could be done. And yet, he failed where I succeeded. Why?

I have pondered this question. Why does one person succeed where another equally skilled person fails? In this case, he possessed superior skills and still failed. I can only conclude that whereas I knew it could be done and was determined to do it, Mike knew it could be done but lacked the determination. Either that, or I was a rock star mountain climber (pardon the pun) my first time out. I don't really believe that to be true. So in the end, I believe that I did it because I knew it could be done and I simply had to do it. Mike didn't have a similar motivation, even in the face of what must have been a humiliating situation for him. Or maybe he was really a lousy climber, who knows? Not every defining moment is poetic.

All these years later, I can still hear Mike imploring me to keep going. And when I run across life circumstances that seem daunting, I remember the lesson I learned that day on the mountain; if you think you can, you can. If you believe it's possible, it is. If you are determined to do it, you will. What is not possible for others is still possible for you, if you believe that it is.

I can't stress this point enough- My obstacle that day was not a sheer granite wall. It was my mind, and my hesitation. Once Mike assured me that it was possible and that I could do it, I did. The only difference between turning back and moving forward was a decision I made in my mind. The mountain didn't care if I went up or down. But I did.

I can't tell you that I always live my life as a fearless warrior since that day, but I can tell you that because I learned that lesson, I have made some pretty bold moves in my life, always anchored in the belief that I have the ability to carry it out. I left a corporate job and started my own business, which has sustained me now for almost 30 years. I jumped out of an airplane at 14,000 feet. I bought rental property and became a landlord. I published a newsletter, and I learned to play guitar and draw portraits. I even became an amateur geologist.

The point here is not to brag about things I have done. The point is that because I learned that all things are possible if you believe they are, I have acted on that knowledge as I move through life, and I have built a happier life as a result.

My wife often invokes the saying "What would you do if you weren't afraid?" It is really a great question, because fear is what stops almost everyone from doing almost everything. There are many talented people in the world who store their talent in their kitchen or basement, or in their head, because they are too scared to bring it into the world.

The difference between doing something new and thinking about doing something new is a very thin line about 100 miles wide. In other words, the idea of writing that book, starting that business, learning to play that instrument may seem daunting, like a 100 mile run. But once you make up your mind to actually stop thinking about it and actually do it, you will discover that it was only a short step away from you all the while. The 100 mile gap was in your head, not in the world.

The voice from the past that still influences me today was an accidental miracle, if there is such a thing. Mike did not set out to teach me a life lesson, and I am not even certain I learned the importance of that lesson until much later. But I believe God opens our eyes when we are ready to see, and what I saw was a way forward in a world full of uncertainty.

I have learned that people who have conquered their fear and achieved greatness are still just people, and still possess fears, doubts and insecurities. I don't think I have ever met a

person who didn't harbor some degree of fear. The only difference between a fearful person who is too scared to try something
new, and a person who has conquered that fear, is a thin line
that is 100 miles wide.

If you really want to do it, you can. That 100 mile gap dis-
appears the instant you make the move from thinking about
it to actually doing it. And that journey always requires that
very difficult first step, which in turn requires you to believe
in yourself, and believe that you can accomplish what seems
impossible, whether it is climbing a granite cliff, starting a business or programming the correct time on your DVD player. If
you think you can, then you can. Mike taught me that lesson
so many years ago.

Tina Torres

Professional Networker, Gratitude Specialist, Entrepreneur Mentor

Tina is a professional networker, entrepreneur, mentor and author who has consulted with corporations, small businesses, and business people across the nation. She is an expert at helping business professionals connect with their target market.

Tina launched her Direct Sales career in 2005 as consultant for Pampered Chef. It was there where she honed her skillsets in sales, team building, and leadership. In 2009, she expanded her personal brand by serving as President of Professional Networking

Connections Savannah for three years.

In her current role as the Gratitude Specialist, Tina teaches entrepreneurs how to create Top of The Mind Awareness, and act on their promptings through heart-felt messages and gifts powered by SendOutCards.

Tina is married, has 3 teenagers, and resides in Kennesaw, GA. For consultation or

speaking engagements, please contact her at tina@thegrati-
tudespecialist.com

You can also get more info on her website at www.thegrat-
itudespecialist.com

Tina's Voice

Sending Out to Give

Tina Torres

prompt·ing
'präm(p)tiNG/
noun
noun: prompting
The action of saying something to persuade, encourage, or remind
someone to do or say something

How many times have you ignored your inner voice, or your intuition? I am talking about that strong feeling that prompted you to take some kind of action.

I never knew what the true meaning of prompting meant until I met Kody Bateman, CEO and founder of Send Out Cards. He founded his company based on a prompting he heard but didn't act on.

Many years ago he was moving out of state when he saw his brother in the distance. He had a prompting to go say good-bye to him and give him a hug, but he was in a hurry, so he did not act. Sadly, a short while later his brother passed away. Kody was filled with guilt, even though he could not have known it was going to be the last time he saw his brother alive.

He vowed that in the future, he would always act on those promptings, and he dedicated his life to teaching, showing, and educating others how to do the same thing. Since 2003 he has stood firm, and remained true to that promise to help millions act on their promptings, and show them how to send positive feelings into the world, and have gratitude in their hearts.

I met Kody Bateman just 30 days after joining the business of Send Out Cards. We met in Fort Lauderdale Florida, where I went to my first "Treat Em Right" seminar. We barely had enough money to travel there, but we made it happen. We brought our own food instead of going out to eat like everyone else. During the lunch session we found a nice quiet spot to eat our sandwiches, and take in all we had learned. We immediately knew we loved this company and the ideals it stood for. We walked around the corner to eat on a bench. It was then our life changed. There in front of us was Kody, eating lunch with his wife Jodi. He was munching on sandwiches just as we were, so we started talking to him, and telling him a little about ourselves.

My husband was in the military at the time, and we had three boys. We had been in the company for less than a month. When we told him that my husband was serving in the military, he put his food down, got up, and came over to shake my husband's hand, telling him "Thank you for serving our country. Without you none of this is possible." That is when that "voice" started speaking to me. That is when I realized where I needed to be.

I couldn't imagine the owner of a million dollar company being so open, so honest and real. He asked us if we were going to convention and we said we would have to see if our finances would allow it. He told us he would give us two convention tickets if we promised to go. He also said he wanted us to come by and let him know when we were there. Of course we went, and wow, did we make a grand entrance! It was on that day that the same little "voice" whispered to me "You are on the right path." This was a business my husband and I could do together, and something I would be proud of doing. It made me feel that when I left this world, and was in front of my maker, He would say, "Well done, good and faithful servant". It was then I began my transformation in life.

I just turned the BIG 40, and to this day I often struggle with my purpose in life, and still seek the path God wants for me. I have struggled off and on with depression for many years, and I kept it to myself because I believed that I was the only one with these feelings. I had to force myself to get out and do things, to have lunch with friends, or go to Bible studies. Some days, just getting out of bed was quite difficult. I always put a smile on my face, got dressed in my best outfit and made the best of it. My coping mechanism was going out and doing things for people, meeting new friends, and networking. It helped me forget about the pain I felt inside.

This continued until I learned about "I AM" statements. An "I Am" statement is a positive affirmation that you write down as if it is already happening. You need to be as specific as possible. The more details the better, so you can actually visualize them happening. Kody teaches this at his seminars, and everyone has a few minutes to write them down. He also gives a few people the chance to read them out loud to everyone.

I read my "I AM" statements daily and I sent an "I AM" card to myself so I can keep it handy and re-read it daily. I was determined to get myself to a happy place again, to make a go at this business and to help other women like me know who they are, and what they want to accomplish in life. I was a stay-at-home mom with three active boys, an army wife to my husband, a room mom to both of my younger ones, a soccer mom to my oldest, and I was deep into my women's ministry at church. I volunteered for everything I could, and I was even in five different Bible study groups at the same time. I had just come to know Christ in 2005, and I had this fire and desire to know everything about this guy Jesus and the meaning of His life. I needed to find out who I was, apart from all the other people in my life.

I didn't grow up in a Christian household. I barely knew who Jesus was, and in fact, I didn't really know Him at all. We didn't have a Bible in the house and we never went to church.

I am the oldest of four children, and we grew up in San Diego, California. My dad was serving in the military, and my mom stayed at home. We were a family who really didn't voice our feelings very often. The attitude that I could do anything I wanted, as long as I worked for it, was not familiar to me.

I had been working since I was 13 years old; I always needed and wanted money to buy the things that my mom wouldn't buy for me. I was one of four children, so of course we were on a budget. I knew if I wanted brand named clothes, or wanted something special, I would have to buy it myself.

I always had the burning desire of wanting more for myself. I knew I was meant to be an entrepreneur (although at the time I didn't know what that word meant). I just didn't have anyone there to help me along, or to tell me "You can do this Tina; you got this." Don't get me wrong, my parents were wonderful. They loved me as much as they could, and they helped me when

I needed help. When I had a baby at the age of 19, my parents stepped in and helped me raise my new son. As a single mom, I didn't have any clue about what to do. I had just graduated high school, and this wasn't in the plan. Still, I knew I could do it, but I would need help. My mom and dad both stepped in to help me each day as I went to college, and again at night. They were great parents and still are to this day. They are still married after 41 years, and to me, that is just phenomenal.

I got my first taste of entrepreneurship shortly thereafter. I started my own day care center in my home in Georgia. I was able to stay home with my new baby and my son who by that time was five years old. It was a starting point, but again, I wanted more, something different. I was searching to find it. I wanted to get out and help others who were like me. I wanted to be around like-minded women.

When I met Kody Bateman, it turned my life around. I admired his continued acts of service to his family and the people in his company. He taught us to act on our promptings right away, instead of putting them off. He had millions join in on the "30 days of Gratitude Challenge" and experience life to the fullest.

The "30 days of Gratitude Challenge" is an amazing way to say "thank you" to those people in your life who have been influential, or who have done something for you in a time of need. You are required to send a card every day for 30 days to one of those people that I described. I am on my third year of doing this and it has brought me such joy. People call, text and email to say how grateful they are for me, and that the card I sent came at "just the right time" in their life. Can you imagine making that much of a difference in the world?

Kody speaks and teaches from his heart. He is truly an inspiration to millions. He told us that he sees us doing "BIG things" in our company; He gave us hope in a future we didn't think we would have. He spoke life, positivity and energy into our lives. His affirmations and "I AM" statements have helped many people, including my husband and me, attain their goals. His motto is "The stories of your mind become the stories of your life." Whether your stories are negative or positive is up to you. If you tell yourself "I can't do this," your mind will already begin to focus on the word "can't". If you repeatedly tell yourself "I AM doing this," your mind will think it has already happened, and you will start to believe it. I learned from him that affirmations are the stories you create in your mind, and actions are the fundamentals that you practice. I needed to take action to make my "I AM" statements come to fruition.

Appreciating what you have daily will not only make you a better person, but it will also start a chain reaction. What you send out is what you get back ten-fold. So why not start a movement? Start a daily gratitude journal and write down the things or people you are thankful for, why you are thankful for them, the qualities you love about that person, and the things they do to make you feel loved. If you want to be great at what you do, whatever that is, then start with *gratitude*. Try smiling at someone, and see if they smile back. Try sending a card to all your friends on their birthdays, and see how many you get back on your own birthday. If you stopped sending Christmas cards because they are not reciprocated, start sending them again. I've had many people tell me "Oh, I don't send Christmas cards anymore." Make a promise right now that this year you will send out at least 50 Christmas cards, whether to clients, friends or family. See how many you get back. See who calls you to say "Thank you for the card." Don't just send out to get, send out to give.

When you wake up in the morning feeling grateful for what you have, and for the people in your life, your day will go so much better. With my own actions and ideas, I was able to help so many others by helping the world to become a better place, and by making someone's day a little bit brighter. I am just one person, but I can help at least 100 people in my life, and they can then help 100 others in their life, and so on.

Over the next few years, we thrived in our business. We were on stage during some of the conventions, and we were fortunate enough to go to Kody's house for dinner. We were on a "United We Send" committee which honored every ethnic background in the Send Out Cards family. I was honored to be included on the "Opportunity" DVD, and my husband even got to have lunch with Kody, and drive his Aston Martin. I guess you can say that we really love this company. Kody's words of encouragement have helped me to be a better me, and have encouraged me to continue to grow, even today. They inspired me to know I can do this. I have watched hundreds of people go to seminars and read their "I AM" statements, acting on promptings that they would normally not act on, because of what he taught us.

The words that Kody spoke that day have resonated with my husband and me for years. We knew we needed to make a difference in the world. Kody and his wife Jodi are not only great inspirational leaders in the industry, but they are also our dear friends. They have made me want to help other people, especially women, find their purpose in life, and to find their passion and happiness; I tend to gravitate towards women entrepreneurs.

I love that women tend to help other women out. We network differently, we build each other up, and always want to help in whatever way possible. I started a coaching business to help women in their business and in their personal lives to act on promptings, and to write their goals down as if they have already been reached. In this way, your goals become your reality. The story of your mind becomes the story of your life.

Promptings will inspire and connect you to a new way of living, regardless of whatever storms you might have passed through. Your inspiration might even help others through their storms. The simple law of attraction is this- what you send out, you will get back. Are you sending out to give...or to get?

It is a blessing to be a part of a huge movement, our "30 days of Gratitude Challenge." So many lives have been changed because of it! A grateful outlook is one of the best investments we can make for achieving the happy, healthy lives we desire.

I encourage you to write some of your own "I Am" statements. Write them on 3x5 cards and place them on your bathroom mirror, in your car, or in your purse. You should see and read them three or four times per day. This will empower you to become the person you want to be. Here are a few of mine:

I AM helping thousands around the world know their calling, and their purpose in life.

I AM reaching millions by teaching the power of Gratitude and starting the "30 days of Gratitude challenge".

I AM helping people know who they are, and that they are special and they are someone others are grateful to know.

I AM a sought after and well-known gratitude coach and speaker.

I AM helping Kody in his crusade of acting on promptings and teaching on the power of the "I AM" statements.

I AM helping millions to learn to act on their promptings and not wait until it is too late to tell someone how they feel.

I am forever grateful for my VOICE, Kody Bateman, and his wife Jodi, who to this day continue to inspire me to be a better person, to act on my promptings and to help make a difference in the world. I will forever be grateful to them for speaking greatness into our lives at a time we needed it the most. Who is your VOICE? Who has helped you become the person you are today? Maybe you are the one who is the inspiration. Make a difference in the world today. You'll be glad you did.

Jayne Miller

Jayne Miller resides in Coon Rapids, Minnesota where she brought up her three sons while she worked for 23 years in a law enforcement agency. Jayne was internationally certified as a Crime Prevention Specialist with the police department and was involved in various crime prevention programs, boards, public speaking, and office administration. Jayne then had to overcome many obstacles and face adversities in life when her chronic Lyme's disease progressed to a life threatening stage.

In her quest to regain and understand her health, she partnered with people in the wellness industry and is an independent distributor working with several wellness companies

including nutritional products, essential oils, and a product line of healthy coffee and teas. She is also involved in a video email and conferencing communications company.

Jayne volunteers at Epiphany Catholic Church in various ministries and helps out in their gift shop. She loves to go on religious pilgrimages to national shrines and holy places. Jayne enjoys different writing projects such as journaling and poetry, and she hopes to write children's and inspirational books one day. As much as she loves Minnesota, Jayne has on her goal list to experience what a "warm" winter feels like in a place where the water isn't frozen.

Contact her at: jayne3miller@hotmail.com or jeventbox@gmail.com

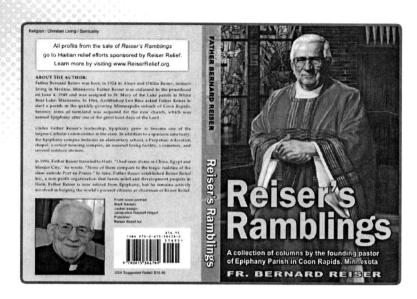

Religion / Christian Living / Spirituality

All profits from the sale of *Reiser's Ramblings*
go to Haitian relief efforts sponsored by Reiser Relief.
Learn more by visiting www.ReiserRelief.org.

ABOUT THE AUTHOR:
Father Bernard Reiser was born in 1924 to Aloys and Ottilia Reiser, farmers living in Medina, Minnesota. Father Reiser was ordained to the priesthood on June 4, 1949 and was assigned to St. Mary of the Lake parish in White Bear Lake, Minnesota. In 1964, Archbishop Leo Binz asked Father Reiser to start a parish in the quickly-growing Minneapolis suburb of Coon Rapids. Seventy acres of farmland was acquired for the new church, which was named Epiphany after one of the great feast days of the Lord.

Under Father Reiser's leadership, Epiphany grew to become one of the largest Catholic communities in the state. In addition to a spacious sanctuary, the Epiphany campus includes an elementary school, a Perpetual Adoration chapel, a senior housing complex, an assisted living facility, a cemetery, and several outdoor shrines.

In 1996, Father Reiser traveled to Haiti. "I had seen slums in China, Egypt and Mexico City," he wrote. "None of them compare to the tragic realities of the slum outside Port au Prince." In time, Father Reiser established Reiser Relief Inc, a non-profit organization that funds relief and development projects in Haiti. Father Reiser is now retired from Epiphany, but he remains actively involved in helping the world's poorest citizens as chairman of Reiser Relief.

Front cover portrait:
Mark Santoli
Jacket design:
Jacqueline Nasseff Hilgert
Publisher:
Reiser Relief Inc

ISBN 978-0-615-36478-0

USA Suggested Retail $18.95

FATHER BERNARD REISER

Reiser's Ramblings

Reiser's Ramblings

A collection of columns by the founding pastor
of Epiphany Parish in Coon Rapids, Minnesota

FR. BERNARD REISER

Jayne's Voice

The German Shepherd

Jayne Miller

Have you ever wondered what comes next when you pass on to eternal life? What might heaven be like? Who might you see there? Will I even make it to heaven? Those thoughts definitely crossed my mind on this day, December 31, 2011 as I dressed for the day's events.

It was a cold, overcast Saturday morning as I drove into the large parking lot of the Church of the Epiphany, one of the largest church parishes in the state of Minnesota and the one I had been a member of for most of my life. This faith community in the center of Coon Rapids grew over the years from an open parcel of farmland into the large church, school, senior housing, assisted living, and extended day childcare facility of today. The grounds include a cemetery, a beautiful national shrine, and prayer gardens as well. All are open to anyone interested in being a part of this holy place.

The founder of this church and all the inclusive buildings on this property was a very faithful servant of God, the Reverend Bernard Reiser. This man had a dream and a vision of creating a faith community that would accommodate the needs of every stage of life from the very young to the aged. I guess you would call it a 'one stop shop' faith community.

Reverend Reiser had retired many years ago, but he still lived in housing on the grounds. "I don't intend to retire," he said. "As long as I can work I will. As long as you can work why sit around gathering dust?" He continued to be an integral part of the community until he lost his struggle with an aggressive brain tumor on December 27, 2011. He was the reason I was driving back into the church lot today. I needed to honor him, and be a part of his funeral. I was glad to see he would be laid to rest in the peaceful cemetery and beautiful grounds he himself had created.

As I turned off the car, I glanced around and saw the streams of people flowing in and out of the entry doors, as they had been all night long.

Father Reiser (as he was most commonly referred to) was given a 24 hour wake for viewing, complete with an honor guard of members from the Knights of Columbus, who kept watch over him with their swords and feather plumed hats. The lines were steady, and people came from around Minnesota and neighboring states to pay their last respects. I had gone during the night to pay my last respects, and to view one last time this man whom I loved and admired with every part of my being.

Upon entering the sanctuary, I gasped at the line that circled the entire room, as each person waited patiently to view the casket at the front of the church. Wow! It seemed like I was witnessing a procession for someone important like the Pope! But then again, he *was* important to us! He had led his church flock in a grand manner and with great wisdom. In doing so, he acquired the nickname of *The German Shepherd.*

I stepped to the side to view the memorabilia table and the pictures. The many items placed here immediately brought tears to my eyes. Oddly, at the same time, a smile broke across my face. I stood there, motionless, as I found my mind transported back in time to when I first met this German Shepherd, who to me was just the pastor at our new church. Yet, he was unlike any other pastor I had ever known.

Imagine this- I'm sitting in the Sunday pew in my Sunday best outfit. I have always been very short. Being short doesn't allow for much of a view from the pew when tall adults are sitting in front of you. So most of my experience back then was listening to "the voice". Father Reiser's voice was a bit stern with a hint of gruffness to it. I wasn't sure what to make of him yet. After we heard the readings of the day and it was time for him to present his homily lesson, there was a lengthy pause. *"Where did he go?"* I wondered. Soon, he appeared coming down the aisle, pushing a casket to the front of the church. Oh my! I was confused for a moment. I thought this was Sunday mass, not a funeral.

The voice then began to speak. The room was quiet and still, and all were listening with anticipation. I thought to myself, *"I better listen."* He certainly had my attention on this one! The point of having the casket and his talk was to teach me about priorities in life. I learned that in death, our material goods won't do us much good. I can't take those bank accounts, homes, cars and boats with me, or pull any of it behind my casket to the cemetery. The really important things are the unseen attributes, such as my spiritual condition—had I lived right, had I served God through serving others? Had I loved others without judgement, and had I shared what I had with those in need? Did I ever embarrass the family name? Could I leave this earth with a clear conscience and sound integrity, and be ready, without a doubt, to meet the Lord? The casket visual worked. I listened and I learned. I still remember what he said that day. He taught well from the pulpit, and I enjoyed "the voice" on Sundays.

I also saw pictures and notes on display from students in the school. Ah, yes, the school days! I was an elementary aged child when I moved to this town. I was blessed to have been able to attend this school in sixth grade, when they finally wrenched open a spot for me. I remember when Father Reiser came to our classroom each week to teach us lessons. I could see him much better in a classroom setting and got to know the person that went with the voice now.

I saw up close the features of this man I couldn't see from my church pew. I got to experience the firm (and I do mean firm) handshake that he was so well known for. He had very large hands, maybe owing to his German family heritage, or maybe from growing up on a farm with chores that required them, I wasn't sure which. Make no mistake; I did learn that I should greet people with good eye contact and offer a solid handshake to let them know I was happy to greet them. I, for my own safety, learned that when you saw the hand of Father Reiser extending out toward yours, you had better brace yourself from head to toe and get ready for the "grip". I have always extended a firm hand-shake since then. I do laugh to myself whenever I encounter a weak or wishy-washy handshake from someone I meet, thinking to myself how they would *not* pass Father Reiser's standard on how to properly shake a hand.

I learned a lot of life lessons beyond reading, writing, and arithmetic when Father Reiser came to my class. He told us stories about growing up on the farm, and doing chores without grumbling about it. We heard his perspective on how obeying his mother and father at all times was a given, not an option; and not going to church on Sunday was not even a consideration unless you were really sick, or better yet, dying. And yes, you went to church even if you had to walk in a blizzard to get there. We learned the *Ten Commandments* and how to apply them to our households, and how to use them in our day-to-day lives.

Father Reiser liked to use visual aids during sermons at school. I recall a time when the whole school was called to the church, and each class filled in the pews by class order. When all were present, Father Reiser came in and sat in a chair in front of the assembly of students. There was another empty chair placed in front of his. When he spoke it was in his stern, but at the same time, caring voice. He asked for a volunteer to come forward and slap him in the face. The room fell silent. Again he asked for a student to come forward and slap his face. No one budged.

With sadness in his stern voice, Father Reiser then explained the reason for this request. Some students had engaged in some mischief and had penciled graffiti on the walls of a bathroom, and threw wet wads of toilet paper all over the walls. Father Reiser told the students that since he was the owner of the building, this action hurt him personally. Making a mess and damaging his property hurt him the same way as if he had been slapped in the face by whoever had done this. He asked us what he had done to make someone so angry and disappointed in him that they felt they had to make a mess of his property. Then he paused. A heavy, uncomfortable silence hung over the room. His point on vandalism had been conveyed. Then he asked for some volunteers to   lp clean up the mess. This time, there were many students that rushed forward. His voice softened as he thanked them for stepping up to help.

This German Shepherd guarded his flock well, and taught them good life lessons not only by textbook, but also by his own example. He used the famous teaching of Saint Francis of Assisi very well, "Preach the gospel always, and if necessary use words."

My eyes next focused on a large, colorful desktop phone modeled after the *Peanuts* character "Snoopy". Father Reiser loved that phone and it was a fixture on his office desk for many years. Again I smile at the memory of the many occasions as an adult that I would sit opposite that desk when meeting with him. I now thought of him more as a mentor than a teacher, although I never stopped learning from him. No matter how crazy his schedule was, he could always find some time to fit you in for a chat. His phone would often ring as you sat there; I don't know how he kept up. He did teach us as youngsters to always eat a good breakfast to provide enough fuel for our day, and I'm thinking he must have eaten quite a lot to keep up his pace.

As you sat in his office you'd marvel at all the books and trinkets he had everywhere, filling every open space on the shelves and counters. Most were gifts he received from people all around the state and beyond.

Did I mention how once you met him you would never forget him? He would not forget you either. He had an uncanny memory for most of his years. I was filled up with the compassion, support, and wisdom contained within those office walls. I emptied his tissue boxes with my tears, and laughed at his wit and jokes. I got refueled by his counsel and found hope in his words when I had none to draw on. I planned for a wedding there, and was counseled through a difficult divorce. I was never judged, but

rather, loved. I was never condemned, but rather, supported. His voice kept me grounded, and his voice kept me sane.

As my eyes continue to scan the items laid out for the wake, I now came across his prayer book, all tattered and worn, and his book with the prayers he used when praying with the sick. I reach out and touch these books and I feel warmth go through me. These books were in his hands almost every day of his life. I have had some struggles with illness over the years, and I had Father Reiser pray with me for healing and strength. He was always such a comfort, and his powerful prayers gave me such peace inside.

Father Reiser had a famous saying, "No one is ever guaranteed tomorrow. You could get hit by a bus when you leave here today and it'd be all over for you. You never know when it's your time. Use your time wisely today. Trust in the Lord always and He will lead you." No matter the situation, he had sound advice.

There are photos on the table of happy wedding couples standing beside Father Reiser. Some of his best sermons came during wedding ceremonies. He really gave good counsel to the bride and groom. The funniest moment was watching their faces when he told them that "today will be the worst day of your lives together." He meant that each day forward should be better than the day before. He would also require them to honor their commitment and celebrate not just on their annual wedding anniversaries, but monthly as well, with special gestures such as flowers for her, and for him, maybe his favorite dessert.

KEEP THE WHEEL TURNING is the heading on a poster I see near the table for Father Reiser's annual fundraising event for his foundation, Reiser's Relief, Inc. This foundation came about after Father Reiser went on a mission trip to Haiti. He returned saying "You can't walk away from misery like that and do nothing." It touched his heart so deeply to see these poor people that he immediately founded Reiser's Relief. The work he has done in Haiti is amazing. He built shelters, schools and feeding stations. He brought in some trucks to bring fresh water to the areas that have no access to clean water. The photos of him with the little children, the elderly, and the homes they built will make you cry. It became his mission to help out in Haiti. He received a grievous wound while he was there, and suffered with the effects the infection it caused. He said the pain kept fresh in his mind that these people needed help. Even when he was diagnosed with a brain tumor, he continued to campaign for more volunteers to help out, in order to keep the wheel turning for Haiti after he was gone.

Each week in our church bulletin there was a column that he titled *Reiser's Ramblings,* in which he would share cute stories, cartoons and lessons as only he could. A book has been made with a compilation of some of those *Ramblings.* The cover on the book is from a print of the same oil portrait done of Father Reiser by his friend and parishioner Mark Sanislo. The original portrait hung in the foyer at Epiphany Church for many years. All the proceeds from this book go to Reiser's Relief for Haiti. His voice will continue on through his book. Readers will be touched for years to come, and Haiti will be blessed.

As I tear up seeing all these memorable items which are flooding me with my own memories, I see the one item that stands out the most. You can't miss it on the table- Father's personalized license plates. You probably never noticed them on the road, however, since he was always whizzing by in a cloud of dust on his way to another call of someone in need! The plate

136

read "XELLENT." This was the notorious reply you would give when Father Reiser asked you, "How are you?" "How's it going?" Anyone not in the 'know' would answer "fine" or "good". That was not what he expected. Father wanted a resounding "EXCELLENT!" Again, he would say to always put forth your best and don't settle for just "good" or "fine". Be "excellent".

It was quite an experience to be at some large function when, from the microphone, that familiar voice would ask the familiar question and the place would erupt in a thunderous "EXCELLENT!" He once put on his business cards, *"Have an excellent day, it beats the alternative."* His humor was infectious.

Ah, what a completely faithful servant of God this man was! Today I feel privileged and humbled to be able to share *my* voice—a very small gift I have to offer, alongside the voices of the massive choir that was assembled especially for this funeral, in honor of this humble and remarkable man. We will sing *"How Great Thou Art"* in closing since that was his favorite song. How fitting—for it could also be applied to this man whose voice had a great impact on all who heard it.

Back to my earlier thoughts: What will heaven be like? Who will I see there? Will I make it to Heaven? I hope it will be EXCELLENT, I hope I will see FATHER REISER, and I CERTAINLY want to be there!

In the meantime, I am grateful to have had this inspirational pastor, teacher, mentor and friend whom I will truly miss. But his voice will never be gone, since I have it forever recorded in my heart.

Myraio L. Mitchell Sr.

When your job is your passion and your career is your calling, you just love what you do. Loving your daily work makes it easy to serve others and that's just what Myraio Mitchell does as President and CEO of New Level Consultants. He serves others by taking one of life's biggest obstacles, a budget, and turns it into something achievable. So many people live beyond their means by being in debt over their heads and it often lands them underwater. Myraio has a way about him, a way of coaching others towards developing a budget and living within that budget and making them want to do just that at the same time.

Stemming from a corporate career mixed most recently

 with helping to facilitate a mega-ministry, Myraio brings a vast spectrum of knowledge and experience to his clients. His skill set includes retail product development and distribution, event planning and logistics, as well as his designation as a trained Financial Coach through Dave Ramsey's Financial Peace Program. Myraio's key motivation

is to change not just his clients' behavior, but their hearts, and to provide hope for them to live by design and not by default.

Contact Myraio:
President & CEO
New Level Consultant, LLC
OffIce: 678-971-9772
www.newlevelconsultants.biz
Info.newlevelconsultant@gmail.com

Myraio's Voice

The Spoken Silence

Myraio L. Mitchell, Sr.

The Casket

Her hands were so cold, yet warmed up the insides of what was left empty and abandoned. Standing there alone, I was motionless. The last scent of Estee Lauder remained in my memory as only a passing fragrance. The colorless glare of the tips of her eyelids, no more to see the gaze of beauty, or offer comfort and protection that once was there during my time of need. No tears to touch the pink and white lace dress that she lay down in. Thoughts of hurt, pain and emptiness engulfed my mind, my emotions, and my body. All I felt were her hands, so cold- her warm touch was no more.

I remember holding her, touching her, and feeling the firm squeeze of her warm hands of protection. As a child, I would visit my Mom on Fridays at her job at the middle school. She was a dietician for the Atlanta Public School system. My dad drove me to see her, and I would jump out of the car, run in, and see my Mom's co-worker and friend at the front desk. She would smile and say, *"Oh, you're here to see your Mom, Mrs. Mozell?"* I would give her a nod and continue on my way to her office in the cafeteria. I was so excited, and looked forward to her smile and the treats she always had for me. She greeted me with a hug and kiss as she took my hand and ask *"How's my baby?"* I replied *"I'm good, do you have anything for me today?"* She would nod her head and hand me my favorite peanut butter cookies with some chocolate milk.

As I nibbled, we talked about our day and she would tell me about her health. Many days she did not feel well. She complained of a headache, which made her very tired. I was concerned about her, but was always glad that she was well enough for us to enjoy each other's company.

As the days flew by, my sister, Valerie and I spent as much time as possible reflecting on life with her. During leisure times at home, we played games like Family Feud. Mom would eat her favorite snack—Hershey's chocolate with almonds—and drink Pepsi Cola. Whenever she was about to win a game of checkers, she smiled from ear to ear and said *"Katy bar the door,"* which meant that we were in trouble and she was about to win the game.

I reflected on those moments as I looked down upon her lifeless body. No more smiles, no more laughter, no more picnics or trips to the park. Every moment with her was a teachable lesson that I took with me, and used to make choices in my life. She taught me and molded me with lessons that would guide me through my life. Foreseeing a future that God had for me, she always told me, *"Stand strong, be happy by being the person God called you to be. No one has a heaven or hell to put you in, so whatever you do is between you and God. Your destiny is one that only you can see, with a vision that you have, let God see you through."*

Sadly, the day came when she told us about her sickness. It was a Saturday afternoon; the weather was calm and the sun was shining brightly on a spring day. Mom and Dad gathered the family in the living room. The room was quiet and still. I had no clue as to why we all were gathered around. I was young and fidgety, waiting for whatever news was to come. I watched as his lips moved, but I couldn't clearly hear what he was saying.

After a few minutes, the words filtered across the room, echoing from wall to wall. *"Live, die or vegetative…"* I had to scramble my brain and quickly process what Mom and Dad were saying to us. *"The doctors found a tumor the size of a grapefruit that was lodged between Mom's left temple and brain. The CAT scan revealed a serious condition, with a 50/50 chance that she would live or die, or wind up in a vegetative state. What do you think about that? What do you think we should do?"* they asked.

Sadness was in the air, no more fidgeting, the words were spoken, but yet I did not understand what was being said. *"What does that mean?"* I thought. *"What was going to happen to us?"* Tears flowed down the faces around me as this overwhelming sadness filled the room. I did not cry; I did not understand what was happening around me. All I knew was that my mom was not feeling well and something was going to happen. I watched my Dad hold my Mom as she talked to us. Dad led us into prayer. *"Dear Heavenly father, please give us strength, I pray that you give the doctors wisdom and knowledge as they go through this surgery, we ask that you strengthen us as a family, strengthen Mozell, please protect her when she goes through this surgery………."*

As he kept praying to God, I could not understand the magnitude of what was to come. And still, there were no tears. His words drifted off during that prayer, only to hear my Mom's voice who started praying. *"God if you let me live to see my baby graduate from high school, I would be extremely grateful. Heal me and help me make a full recovery........"* I listened to Mom pray for herself, for the family, but most of all for me. She asked to live through her agony and pain, through her surgeries, for my sake. She wanted more for her baby, for me. I had to be strong. I had to be there for her no matter what the odds were, or what it cost me in life. I had to take care of my Mom.

My days of innocence and childhood were gone. I had to grow up quickly, leaving behind my playful thoughts and childish ways. My Dad told us we had to take on new roles and responsibilities around the home, things that Mom would have normally have done. Mom had already taught us cooking, cleaning and household duties. Now we had to perform. Both me and my sister became even closer, and I called her "Mama Val."

I could only process what was happening right then; her thoughts, her inspirations, her touch of serenity. We created a special bond. Mom went through many surgeries, and after every surgery I walked into her hospital room to find tubes and beeping monitors, the scene of a mechanical motherboard supporting the life of one being. It was a room that people sought hope and answers. A room that endured life and death. A room that walked through happiness and sadness. As she lay there, I walked over to her and found her hands under the cold white sheets.

I leaned over to her and said, *"Hi Mom, it's me."* She opened her eyes and squeezed my hand. This was a moment of *"The Spoken Silence."* This was our special moment where she told me she was ok. The strength remaining in her weak body gave me strength and energy to have hope, and I was assured that she had another moment, another day to see me grow up.

The thought of her very first surgery was scripted in my mind. I felt hurt, pain and anger, but still had no tears. I remember my Dad holding my hand and walking me to the chapel of the hospital. The lights were dim and the room was peaceful. He wanted us to talk to God about Mom. We nestled together and kneeled. He looked me in the eyes and said *"Son, it's okay for a man to cry."*

I thought to myself, I am a boy, a man, a child of God. I do not cry, I do not weep. I need to be strong for him, I need to be strong for her.

These thoughts played in my head and as I looked over at my Dad. For the first time I saw this strong Man of God cry. This man who worked all the time, this man who empowered us, this man who never let his emotions get the best of him, was sobbing. His tears flowed down his cheek, as his body curled over with an overwhelming feeling of sorrow and pain. At that moment I felt free to hurt, free to feel what was bottled up inside, free to understand that it was okay to not be strong all the time. If my Dad could weep, then it was okay for me to weep, because our Heavenly Father wept.

From Father to Father and Father to Son, we are all made in His image. *(John 11:33-35: "When Jesus saw her weeping, and the Jews who had come along with her were also weeping, he was deeply moved in spirit and troubled. "Where have you laid him?" he asked. "Come and see, Lord," they replied. Jesus wept."*

There was no question about what I needed to do for her, and for the family. There were many times of taking mom back and forth to doctors' appointments, testing, rehabilitation, and assisting with medication. My ambitious mind guided me to do what I believed was right. *Philippians 2:3 "Do nothing out of selfish ambition or vain conceit. Rather, in humility value others above yourselves."* I enjoyed the last moments that we shared with Mom. Although she always made a full recovery after surgery, allowing her to return to normal activities of cooking and cleaning, the tumors always came back, which led her to many more surgeries. She never gave up and had faith that she would be ok.

It was a Friday night 14 years later, after her fifth surgery. She was recovering well, but I had to work overnight. I called Mom to tell her that I was coming to see her the next morning after my shift was over. My sister Valerie answered the phone, and passed along the message to Mom. As they talked back and forth, I could hear her saying *"OK, I'll see you in the morning."* She sounded happy and that made me content.

I finished my shift and went home to get changed. I went to pick up my Dad at his home so we could drive to the hospital together. As I walked into the house, the room was silent and still. Both Dad and my sister were sitting at the kitchen table. They locked eyes with me. *"We have been trying to reach you, we left you several messages."* My heart raced, my blood burned through my skin with fear of the unknown. *"Mom is in a coma. We can't see her until 11."* I asked myself *"What did that mean? Is this the end? She said she would see me in the morning, this morning!"* I could not process what I was feeling. My body became numb, and I was hurting and fearful. I needed to see her. I realized at that moment, at 21 years old, that I had heard her voice for the last time. We gathered together and made the journey to the hospital.

As we stepped into the ICU (intensive care unit), I stood there looking at her. *"Why God?, Why does this have to happen to this virtuous women? Why does she have to go through this pain? Please keep her alive and heal her."* As these thoughts ran though my head. I questioned Him, and I questioned my relationship with Him. "What can I do?" There was nothing to do. She was gone. Gone to be with the one who took her away from me.

As my hands held hers at that very moment, there was no warmth, there was no energy animating her touch. Her hands were cold and motionless. She laid there as I stood by her bedside, looking, waiting for a smile, a moment of breath to fill the room. I waited, staring at my best friend. I wanted her to wake up. I called out for her, telling her *"Mom it's me, your baby."* She didn't respond.

It was then, the remembrance of her that bought me to this day, in October 1990. This moment of me looking at her in the casket as she slept peacefully in the arms of an angel.

The Inspiration

In 1995, I heard "The Spoken Silence," I was going through a game of life that I called "CHANCE." Now you see, I was always raised in the church, always loved the Lord and always knew I was protected under His wings. My Dad is a pastor and I knew about trusting God and following His guidance. This time, I was hearing the Lord talk to me about my job vs. my spirituality. He called upon me to leave my financially stable corporate position. I knew I was being called into full-time ministry, but I didn't see the vision clearly. I was trying to understand what it was, but there was no more guidance, only silence. "What does this mean?" I thought to myself.

Sometimes in our lives we will encounter silence. This is moment when we may feel that we desperately need to hear from God, but we don't feel His presence. We may even feel that He has left us all alone. This is where Jesus teaches "believe in me!" even if it seems as if nothing is happening. He teaches us that when we cannot hear Him, we need to open up our Bible and read His word. We need to trust God and have faith that He will truly be there for us in times of desperation and need. God's word will guide us to listen clearly to his faith and love.

On a Saturday morning in June of 2000, my battle of decision was over, only for a new one to begin. I was driving home to where the highway came to a split. I looked to my right, and a Chevy S-10 pick-up truck passed with a bumper sticker reading- Isaiah 41: 10-13. The bumper sticker appeared as big as a billboard. Was this a sign? What does this mean? When I got home I looked it up and read: *"So do not fear I am with you, do not be dismayed, for I am Your God. I will strengthen you and help you. I will uphold you with my righteous right hand...For I am the Lord your God who takes hold of your right hand and says to you do not fear I will help you."*

That Monday morning, I turned in my resignation. I made my decision. I worked my final two weeks trusting in God and all that He had designed for me. Financially we were set which made it a bit easier, and I wasn't worried. I enjoyed my family time and didn't let anything worry or distract me. I believed that this was all His plan.

As time went on, I was now working in full-time ministry as a part of the facility maintenance team. I began to realize that there were not enough funds to live the lifestyle I was accustomed too. My financial situation was suffering, and I used all the money from my savings and investments. I cashed in all of my 401k accounts to offset the cost of my monthly expenses.

Within three years the money I had saved was almost depleted. Bill collectors, repossessions and foreclosure notices were hitting my mailbox. I took on a second full-time job overnight to supplement my income, but still it was not enough to cover the monthly expenses. Because of the pressure, I chose to file for chapter seven bankruptcy. At times I would not eat, and took this time to fast and pray for God's direction and wisdom, so I could make sure that my family was able to eat. There were times when I could not pay the utility bill and keep the lights on and I had to prioritize which bills I would pay. My family was now living paycheck to paycheck, and I struggled from the pit of my stomach. I kept this away from my family and co-workers; I couldn't let them see me like this. I had too much pride.

I heard my mother's voice: *"Never tell anyone your business, and if you keep your mind on Him and not on earthly things and stay focused then, you can accomplish anything."* These words kept me going. Between my mother's words and my trust in God, I could not give up or give in. I also remembered this verse: Deuteronomy 31: 6 *"Be strong and courageous, do not be afraid or terrified, because of them, for the Lord your God goes with you, he will never leave you nor forsake you."* It was "the Spoken Silence" of the spirit of God. He was speaking to me at this moment. God continued working on me as I had faith in His words and His promise that he would never forsake me. He had a design mapped out for me. Jeremiah 29:11 *"For I know the plans I have for you," declares the* LORD, *"plans to prosper you and not to harm you, plans to give you hope and a future."*

The Omnipresent

Life took me on a journey to bring me to where I am today. In life, I am strategically placed in a design that was mapped out for me. I live by design, not by default. My financial situation went from the low rocky roads into the valleys of the high mountains and is still climbing. Now I am able to serve people and help families in need with my new consulting firm "New Level". "New Level" began as a thought, turned into a vision, and is now a reality, as I am live my dream based on faith and belief. I needed faith and belief to accomplish all that I have done in my life. We need to reach a New Level in our lives, not falling back on what was, but focusing on what is; a level of reaching new heights of accomplishment.

"New Level believes that every individual and organization has their own unique story to tell; sometimes they just need help express- ing it. Isaiah 43:19 *"See, I am doing a new thing! Now it springs up; do you not perceive it? I am making a way in the wilderness and streams in the wasteland."*

God has allowed me to meet great people. This paradigm shift in my life has allowed me to be in complete harmony with my emotions, thoughts and vision. I feel my mother's spirit around me everyday as I work my way through life's decisions. She has transcended her spirit within human form and walks with me everyday. I can feel her in my heart and hear her voice in my thoughts. With the warmth of her hands I am able to feel again. I no longer feel lost living each day. I feel alive through her. I am able to live life on my terms, while helping others in the process of my journey. I can climb any mountain with her spirit beside me, there is no ocean that is too big for me to swim. She guides and protects me from the lightning, and holds my hand through the storm. She has spoken and I can hear her voice through "The Spoken Silence."

Kathleen Walker Hughes

I was born and raised in Buffalo, N.Y. so I'm a Yankee by birth. We moved to Atlanta in 2000, so I'm only Southern by real estate!

I have been married for 38 years. We have been blessed with 11 children, and as this goes to print are expecting our 12th grandchild.

It goes without saying that my career has been in Domestic Engineering. I chose to be an at-home mom. I also chose to home school six of my children for four years.

Losing both of my parents to degenerative diseases when I was a young mother is what fueled my passion to learn as much as possible about preventative health. I want to live a long full life enjoying the grandchildren, great grandchildren, and their children.

I became a passionate, purposeful, and professional advocate for health and wellness, helping people attain and maintain a healthy lifestyle. I want to leave a legacy of generational health.

I wake up everyday with a grateful heart. I thank God for the opportunity to touch and empower as many lives as possible.

Contact me at: www.kathleenhughes.juiceplus.com

kathleen4health@gmail.com

Kathleen's Voice

A Friend Speaks to the Soul

Kathleen Walker Hughes

Twenty-eight years ago I stood on top of a volcanic crater looking down into the aqua blue waters of the Pacific Ocean. It was an incredible site. An immense feeling of awe came over me as I viewed the magnitude of His creation. In stark contrast to that beauty was the realization that at one time, there was a massive eruption of molten lava where I was standing. The fast moving, fire red lava streamed down the flanks of the volcano, destroying any sign of life in its path. In the aftermath, as the years passed, the hard black rock decayed, and spilled it's nutrients onto the landscape. Plant and animal life sprang into existence once more.

How can something so chaotic and destructive produce life again? It is the power of God to bring renewal, and He most certainly brings restoration into our lives. My story is about renewal and how my friend's voice brought courage and faith into my life, especially during the darkest times. We all go through pain and sorrow, but the presence of God, in the form of a friend, is like a warm comforting blanket. It can shield us and protect us, and allow the deep inner joy to surface, even in the most challenging circumstances.

It was the voices of my parents that spoke into my life during my early years. They taught, guided and corrected me, but they also encouraged me during stressful times, when life seemed most uncertain.

The middle and high school years had their share of emotional times, and I needed a few good friends to help survive those challenges. Girls have a lot to deal with during these crazy years; hormones, boys, breakups, and most importantly, what clothes to wear! These issues seem to dominate our lives as teens. I'm thankful for the friendships and how they helped me to weather those few chaotic years, and to somehow find joy in the journey.

After I left high school, I attended a two-year Business School for no particular reason. My real goal was to get married and be a mother. Bill and I had been dating off and on throughout high school. I was a freshman when we met, and we had the same circle of friends. I was actually dating his best friend Paul, and after Bill would drive him home, it only made sense that we would spend some time together.

And that is how it all began. I completed Bryant & Stratton Business School when I was 19. Bill and I became close friends with a family that was looking to "go back to the earth", and we decided to become a part of that journey with their family. It turned into quite an adventure. We purchased an old school bus and turned it into our traveling home for our move to the mountains. There were twelve of us that made the big move, and Bill and I were married in those Ozark Mountains. It was the tail end of the hippie era, so that type of wedding was reminiscent of the lifestyle. All of us had long hair and flowers everywhere. We went back to the earth, and back to nature in a very interesting way! There were some similarities to Little House on the Prairie; cows, chickens, and no indoor plumbing. It was simplicity at its best. It actually brings a smile to my face thinking about it right now. There were no phones to be found, as cell phones were non-existent, along with computers and all of our other daily technology. And we were happy without it!

As I entered adulthood, I sought out friendships that would resonate with my own voice. The voice that changed everything in my life was that of my best friend Lonny Hanes. I was 24 years old and had just had my first baby, when my husband and I decided to attend a Full Gospel Businessmen's event to hear Dave Roever, a Vietnam war hero. As I looked around, I noticed one of my high school friends, Mark Hanes. He introduced me to his wife Lonny. She had a warm smile and a great sense of humor. These are two qualities that easily invite a friendship. Lonny and I are actually somewhat opposite in our personalities. She can speak easily with boldness, but in love. I would describe her as an otter/lion personality. I have more of the golden retriever personality. The otter type person is one who always looks for fun; the life of the party! The lion part is their boldness. My golden retriever, by contrast, loves life and fun, but is somewhat more reserved about it. They always want to be kind no matter what. Boldness is not a part of their personality. They say opposites attract in marriage, and I believe it is also the same in friendship

Why did Lonny's voice make such and impact in my life? The number one reason is honesty. I remember conversations we had when I was going through troubling times, and having a pity party for myself. Lonny had the unique ability to pull me out of my slump by speaking truth with love and grace, even if my feelings were hurt. That is how a friend ministers to your heart.

We both had our first three children around the same time. That certainly made for many entertaining experiences. We worked through exhaustion due to sleep deprivation, endured the challenges of breastfeeding, and had foggy brains on a regular basis. Our sons were best friends, as were our daughters. Together we saw our children through Royal Rangers and Missionettes, dating and proms. While Lonny stopped at three children, I went on to have seven more! Through all that she remained my friend. She even gave me a baby shower when I was expecting my tenth baby. Not many women get a shower at that point, but then again they don't have a friend like her. Breast feeding, constantly changing diapers, and having to put little ones down for naps can curtail your freedom. Nonetheless we enjoyed a sweet fellowship at our church and watched our children grow up together.

Amidst the joy of raising children, there were times of sorrow and pain. I vividly remember the afternoon phone call telling me that Mark's brother Greg had been killed in a motorcycle accident. It was a time of grief and sorrow. Being there for them, caring for the children, bringing meals, and praying with them while they were healing, is what friends instinctively do. It was heartbreaking for Mark and his parents. They had only had two sons, and now Mark was their only son, and he was without a brother.

Some of our other storms were the result of prodigal children. Navigating their way through the teen years was a time of great challenge. The choices they made were not always reflective of the values they were taught. There were many sleepless nights praying in the darkness for their safety. Thankfully our husbands shared our burden. Bill, Mark, Lonny and I spent a lot of time encouraging one another. It was very painful to watch your children make choices that brought devastation into their lives. You never imagine while you are rocking one of them to sleep, that someday you will be visiting them in jail, or a hospital, due to the poor choices they made.

When it comes to mothers, our hearts beat differently for our children. They yearn; they cry out, they also seek refuge with a special friend. More times than I can count, Lonny has prayed with me. I do not remember any exact words, but what I do remember is the power, love, and sincerity of her prayers; prayers that healed our hearts. We are to rejoice with those who rejoice, and weep with those who weep. Our friendship has doubled our joy and divided our grief.

There have also been some very special times that will forever be cherished. In the fall of 1987 the four of us had our first real vacation—a trip to Maui! We had so much fun, and so many incredible memories were made there; snorkeling, exquisite dinners, unforgettable sunsets, and the drive up to Haleakala Crater! Who could forget that very memorable drive up the mountain with all the hairpin turns? We were extremely carsick, but the "green" feeling was quickly replaced with awe as we viewed the Pacific Ocean through the clouds. We were also introduced to the rare Silversword. They only grow on Haleakala. They only bloom once in their life, and then they die. The four of us have a trip back to Maui planned for January 2017 for our 40th Anniversary.

A year following that first trip, I lost my mother. It had been a very difficult three years for her health, prior to her passing on. A massive stroke in 1985 left half her body paralyzed. I had my fifth baby five days after her stroke. It was chaotic to say the least. Then she had a fall that broke her hip, followed by major open-heart surgery. This was an extremely difficult time for our family, as I had to divide my time between a newborn, four other children, and my mom. There was juggling between my two siblings and myself. Lonny's friendship during these difficult years was invaluable. Her voice spoke encouragement and friendship. This is how you know the worth of a true friend.

My mother and I had become closer after I began having my own children. I began then to understand the heart of my mother and how much she had sacrificed for me. We did not have a lot of possessions growing up, but family time and vacations were an important part of our lives. After I married, I would go over to my mom's once a week. There were no deep conversations together, but I knew she loved me and wanted me to have a great marriage and a great life. My parents had divorced after 30 years of marriage. Their divorce became final before the birth of my first child. I was extremely heartbroken, not only for my parents, but also for my children. They would never see my parents together.

When I lost my mother, I grieved for the loss and loneliness in her life. I was hurt deeply watching my parents' marriage dissolve. My father was never the same. When he visited, I saw the brokenness in his eyes. Sadly, six years after my mother's death, my father also had a major stroke…another tragedy. Ironically, I was very pregnant at the time of his stroke. Watching both parents become disabled when they should be enjoying life and grandchildren was crushing. I felt robbed of that relationship.

Life has a way of changing course without much advance notice. In the late summer of 1999 my husband parted ways with the company he had worked with for 21 years. This was totally unexpected, and of course unwanted. We still had ten of our 11 children living at home. There wasn't a lot of time to think about what comes next. We had every intention of remaining in Buffalo. Bill's mom was 82, my dad was 76 and disabled, and our two oldest daughters were attending state colleges there. But it did not take long to exhaust the search in Buffalo. Resumes were sent, and out of state job interviews began. Our house went up for sale. The most promising job looked to be in Atlanta, and after two trips to Dixie, Bill was offered the job. The stress of selling our home and finding the right one in Atlanta began. I flew down on a couple of weekends, and we finally found the right home. It all happened so quickly. It felt as if someone had pressed the fast forward button in our lives.

House hunting suddenly seemed easy compared to the overwhelming task of packing and moving nine of our children. Thankfully, the hustle and bustle of it all kept me focused, allowing me to avoid thinking about the painful separation that was looming on the horizon. How could I leave my best friend? Yes, it hurt to leave our two oldest daughters and other family members behind, but I knew we would be together frequently for holidays. The thought of not seeing my friend Lonny, however, was a different kind of pain.

After all the papers were signed for our new home, I flew to Atlanta to begin the process of locating schools and getting seven of our children registered. Who would come along with me to help with this major task? Yes, my friend Lonny! She always had the ability to take an overwhelming situation like this and make it fun.

The day that I had been dreading finally arrived. We pulled out of our driveway one last time to embark on a new journey, a new chapter in our lives. But that does not happen without painful goodbyes, a lot of tears, and fears of leaving precious things behind.

Our two oldest daughters, Leah and Elisabeth, were there, along with Bill's mom, my dad, our children's youth pastor, and four of our friends; Leroy and Marleen, Mark and Lonny. There were so many mixed emotions. Saying goodbye to our daughters was much different than saying goodbye to my disabled father. There were overwhelming feelings on many different levels. Our teenage children obviously had more difficulty leaving their friends. Changing schools is hard enough, but changing states makes it an even greater challenge.

Arriving at our new home was just as large a task as leaving the old one, if not more so. Where to go and what to do? Crossing the Mason Dixon line brought a little culture shock as well. Living in Buffalo, you only saw a confederate flag in a book. Not so in Georgia. They were on the back of pickup trucks, tee shirts, and hanging on peoples porches! Our kids knew immediately they had arrived in redneck country! I quickly learned that sweet tea, coke and fried chicken were considered core nutrition in the south.

Thankfully, a few weeks after we arrived, Lonny flew down to help me get organized. What a relief to have an organized house and time with my friend! You can never have too much of either one.

It is now 2015. We have lived in Atlanta for 15 years. A lot has transpired in all of our lives since then. We've had both happy celebrations, such as weddings and grandchildren, as well as losses. My father passed away 11 days after our daughter Leah was married, and my brother died in 2010. I loved him so much. He was kind and funny, but he could not overcome his alcoholism. He drank himself to death at the age of 61, the same age and same month that my mother passed away.

I have made a lot of trips up to Buffalo to visit my daughters and grandchildren. It is so important to build those relationships, despite the miles between us. There is less time for Lonny and I to get together now, but it has not had a negative impact on us. When you have built a meaningful friendship over the years, their voice remains in your heart.

That is how you know that the voice has made a difference, and changed you for the better.

A few years after moving to Atlanta I began to homeschool my children. I went to a homeschooling fair to purchase curriculum. Among my many purchases was a brochure from MemLok, a bible memory software program. I called the number on the brochure to get more information regarding this program. I was very impressed and purchased the program to add to our curriculum. I also became very interested in a health and wellness product that would add daily nutrition into our diets. What was really intriguing was their Children's Health Study program, which allowed for children between four through college age to get the product free! Mention 'good nutrition' and 'free' to a mother and see what happens!

To me the word prevention meant a lot. I had lost both parents and my brother. Yes, it was their lifestyle choices that brought about their illnesses, but prevention still makes so much sense for everyone. It only took me a few months to realize that this was something that I had to share. I did not realize at the time I was about to embark on a whole new journey in life, but when God opens a door, it is a wise person who walks through it. He knew what I needed long before I did. That is called divine intervention.

When something new and exciting comes into your life, who do you share it with first? Yes, your dear friend! It most certainly made sense to Lonny, and she is still my client today. I have since gone on to become a Certified Health Coach through the Sears Wellness Institute. I know I'm extremely blessed to be a part of a company with a mission to Inspire Healthy Living Around The World. I wake up every morning with a burning passion and a deep sense of purpose.

God has been so faithful through all the ups and downs in my life. I have learned and grown more through the broken times. I have also learned not to stay silent during these times. Speaking out of your brokenness is powerful. It is truth that will touch and encourage other lives. I have been blessed with a faithful husband, 11 healthy children, and the joy of being a grandma with an abundance of grandchildren. I now have the opportunity to speak into their lives.

I'm grateful for the many voices that have spoken into my life, even the ones that were not so kind or encouraging. Those voices also played their part in growing us into maturity. They help us develop discernment, which we need throughout our lives.

I believe each one of us has a desire for our voice to speak into another person's life and awaken a purpose and a passion that will inspire them to pursue their dreams. I pray that each person reading this will be blessed with an exceptional friend in his or her life, a friend that will touch, change, and speak into your soul as Lonny spoke into mine.

"A friend loves at all times." Proverbs 17:17

Cece Landress

Cece Landress is life-long educator. She enjoys working with people on developing excellence in their lives and overcoming obstacles. She is a motivational speaker and educational trainer. She has started a program called Success Now and is noted for her work in leadership development.

Cece has earned a BA in Psychology from Stetson University, a MAT in Political Science and Curriculum from Emory University, a MTEE from Georgia State and a DAST in Economics and Leadership from Emory University. Her other writings are educational and include Back to Basics, Using Controversial Issues in the Classroom, Playing the Stock Market, Your Financial Future for High School Students, Finding the Leader in You, If Everyone was a Leader, The New Bully, Why Programs Don't Work in Schools, and How to Destroy a Program of Excellence in Five Easy Steps. She also coordinated the Intervention Program for Test Success with teachers known for their excellence in motivating students and teaching.

She is a member of Atlanta Writers and has been distinguished with the Winning Women of Atlanta and Georgia Geography Teacher of the Year Awards. She states her greatest achievement has been the role she has played in raising a daughter who believes in excellence. Cece is a native of Atlanta, GA and is excited to add her Voice to the Voice that Changed Everything. Contact her at SuccessNowForever@gmail.com

Cece's Voice

Life Isn't a Battle, It's an Adventure

Cece Landress

My mother's voice is quiet and calm, but full of courage and patience. She was one who provided loving guidance while allowing you the space and time to think, and figure out your next step. Mom was the one who faced down a gunman intent on robbing and harming her family, who weathered terrible tragedies, and still came out smiling and successful. I don't think she realizes the impact she had on my life by her actions. Quiet voices make a difference if you listen to them. But, I want to say it out loud so you will know this amazing woman.

At an early age, this beautiful petite woman met a man with an entirely different voice. He was a tall good looking man, full of charm and wit. His voice was bold and demanding. His controlling nature provided forceful guidance and protection, as one would expect of a military man.

Although their voices were very different, they collided and ignited a passion that would carry them on a lifelong adventure. It was a fiery, fantastic journey in which their voices would provide balance for each other. Often his demanding manner would go too far and she would have to step up, and quietly reel him back.

Mom found it difficult to say no to those who were in need. Often, as she took on more responsibility, his protective voice emerged. Together, they became a dynamic duo living a life full of highs and lows, full of struggles and joy. They demonstrated their philosophy that no obstacle was so great that it could not be overcome with love and perseverance.

Their unity provided a life that was stimulating and purposeful, even in the midst of troubling times. Early in their marriage, they lost their second son, enduring a heartbreak that never completely healed. Mom vividly remembers begging for help for her newborn. The medical staff claimed her son was fine, but her mother's intuition knew something was wrong. As she helplessly laid in the military hospital bed, the medics refused to listen. When my parents left the hospital, they carried their son's remains in a box, instead of a baby in their arms. My mother still grieves.

Her great strength, a loving husband, and the small arms of her loving first son aided her through the emotional weeks that followed. Over the next few years, they brought another son and two daughters into their home. As the middle child, I wonder how she survived four very active and creative kids.

During the first thirty years of my life, their voices worked in harmony to teach me lessons that have molded me into the person I am today. Playing hard and working hard was the norm. We had incredible weekends filled with family, including cousins and grandparents. However, Monday through Saturday was all business.

They owned several clothing stores designed to meet the needs of the growing professional and social world of men and women in Atlanta. When not in school, all the children were an active part of their business world. We were held to high standards and expectations. No matter the activity, all children were expected to display our best manners and work as a team. Even before starting first grade, I discovered the importance of teamwork.

Communication was essential to being part of a productive team. One day our listening and teamwork paid off. On a sunny Saturday, mom had all of us in her women's clothing store. We were enjoying hot donuts purchased from the local bakery a few doors up the street. Then the phone rang.

Mom cheerfully answered the phone. She heard a man with a deep, gruff voice on the other end of the line. He told her, "Look up. I am in the phone booth across the street. I am watching. I have a gun. Do not try anything."

Calmly she moved us behind the counter and told us, "Stay on the floor and play the quiet game. Do not talk." While this threatening man continued to rant and make lewd suggestions concerning my mom, she remained calm and wrote a note. "Help me. Call the police. I am being threatened by a gunman." As he proceeded to tell her more of his vicious thoughts, she passed the note to my oldest brother and told him to sneak out of the back door and take the note to a neighbor.

He crawled out back into the alley and banged on the doors until someone answered. Handing off the note, he ran back into the shop and crawled back behind the counter. She still had the man with the deep voice on the phone as he proceeded to tell her, "If you want to keep your children safe, do what I tell you. Take all of your money out of the cash register and put it on the counter. I want it now. I am coming for you and the money."

She placed the money on the counter as the gunman stepped out of the phone booth. Sirens were wailing in the distance as we saw approaching blue lights. As policemen stormed the store, she screamed, "The phone booth!" The police turned to see a man running up the hill. The hot pursuit was on to capture this evil man.

Our smart, quick thinking mom saved our lives, even though she lost a little trust in the human race. She showed us that despite one's fears, you must remain calm. Sometimes events like these require changes in your life, and unfortunately, our lives would have to continue outside of school, with a nanny.

Life adventures continued during summer breaks. Each summer, my parents planned an incredible vacation. Our adventures were educational, but they taught us life lessons at the same time. Summer vacations taught me patience, creativity, compassion and risk taking.

One summer vacation, our trip went from coast to coast. Our trek across the nation included four kids under the age of twelve, two parents and a grandmother, all in one car. Traveling was part of the escapade. My parents drove all day and sometimes all night to get to the next place. The baby traveled in the front seat between my parents. In the back, my grandmother had a window seat and the three of us shared the rest of the seat. We played games and read. When it was time to sleep, everyone had a designated place. One brother rested against the door while the other one curled up in the floorboard. I, on the other hand, was the lucky one. I was small enough to sleep in the back, under the rear window.

Our adventure took us over mountains and into deserts. We saw the grandeur of the Grand Canyon, then experienced the excitement of Las Vegas. The highlight of the trip happened in Yellowstone National Park. We watched Old Faithful erupt. Then suddenly, my father stopped the car to have his picture taken with a bear. Being the invincible soul that he was, Daddy walked right up to a bear and started playing with him. Soon he had him up on his hind legs and took the opportunity to hug him. One would have thought they were best friends.

Inside the car, there was chaos. My excited brothers were jumping around at the sight of my dad's new friend. Grandmother was yelling at Dad, while my mother was fuming as she consoled me. The park ranger approached my dad, shaking his head while laughing at his brave antics. "Sir, the bears are wild and you should not attempt to play with them. I guess we need to put up a sign that says, 'Please do not hug the bears!'"

With my brothers cheering my dad on, we continued on our journey (inside the car). As I crawled into the back seat, my overzealous brothers thought it would be fun to bring the bears closer to the car so they could have an up-close and personal experience too. In spite of the "Do Not Feed the Bears" sign, they carefully placed bread in the windows and rolled them up tight. The bears approached the car and stood on their hind legs to reach the food. As I cowered with fear, the bears proceeded to climb on the car. My brothers cheered their accomplishment, but actually, their joy was really in listening to my screams of terror. This was not a good way to learn calmness in the face of fear.

Even though all journeys have some element of risk, you ignore the risk when you meet people in need. The next summer adventure took us to the Island of Hispaniola in the Greater Antilles. I had never been around people who were hungry, without medical care, and alone on disease infested streets. One amazing day brought smiles to many faces. In a walk through town, the streets were filled with unsupervised small children wearing dirty, torn clothes. The houses were open huts. I clung to my mother as my father led the way. He gave money to all the begging kids along our walk. The more money he gave away, the more the kids began to follow us. Soon he looked like the pied piper. When the money ran out, the smiling kids went on their way.

As we continued on our walk, we came upon a ragged man with a long beard who was carving statues. In talking with the man about his art work, the artist admired my father's shirt and told him how he wished he had a new shirt. So my father gave him the shirt off his back. My mother could only smile and laugh. Shirtless, my father proudly carried back a tall primitive carving that the man wanted him to have for good luck. While on life's adventure, all people are important to acknowledge, and you should always be prepared to reach out to people in need.

Back home, each day was an adventure. In first grade, I went to school with my brothers while my parents managed their stores. After school, we walked the twelve blocks home with all the neighborhood kids. Arriving home to a nanny was definitely not exciting, but safety was imperative.

One day everything changed. Our safety and security was stolen from us when we came home from school and no one was there. No nanny. No baby sister. We ran all over the house, down into the basement and out in the yard yelling for the nanny. NO one responded. In a panic, my brother called my parents to tell them no one was home.

After calling the police, my parents frantically raced home. They raced around the house searching for a note, a clue. For something, anything. My sister, her Sunday clothes, coat and hat were missing along with the nanny. Who took the nanny and my sister?

Police cars swarmed the neighborhood. They searched surrounding neighborhoods, hospitals, and streets that led downtown. As dark was approaching, the last downtown bus stopped at the end of the street. The nanny emerged holding the hand of my sister. My sister was dressed in her coat and matching hat in the heat of the day. As the bus pulled away, they slowly began walking down the street to the house. The police swooped in and took the nanny in for questioning in the disappearance of my sister. Our home sanctuary loss some of its security that day.

With my sister home, life began to change. My parents were more protective. Mom sold her dress shop so she could be home with us after school. As always, family was first.

What was their solution to regaining their sanctity and security? They moved us to the suburbs, and eventually to rural Georgia. My vision of the country was comparable to the television show Green Acres. I thought of cows, pigs, chickens and horses. This was going to be some new adventure.

Luckily my parent's vision was a little different. They purchased 40 acres that backed up to a river, with a highway in the front. They built a house and pool in between. It was time for another fun adventure.

The journey to the new house seemed like forever. In this extraordinary place, there were no grocery stores, no houses, and no gas stations. It took 30 minutes on a yellow school bus to get to school. People spoke with unusual accents. I thought I was in a foreign country. I became hopeful when I read "Success Lives Here" on the county water tower, and saw a sign with the city motto "Where Everybody is Somebody". The school was in an old stone building. My mother assured me that moving to a small town was going to be a great adventure. I found the girls in school to be mean. I felt like a NOBODY. I cried for two weeks.

My mom had said it takes time and a positive attitude for change to occur. In the meantime, you have to be your own best friend. So I went to school with a smile and worked hard. Soon things changed. Eventually, this move became the best decision my parents could have made. The mean girls stopped being mean and we all became best friends. In a matter of time, I knew almost everyone. Here was a place where all races and ethnic groups were friends. Everyone was significant. People should be so lucky to have such a unique life experience. Sometimes parents do know best.

Years later as an adult, I learned a very valuable lesson from mom about striking out. Sometimes in life people experience tragedy after tragedy and wonder if life is ever going to get better, or if they are destined to strike out.

I was having an incredible time teaching high school and living a fun life. One evening, I needed dishwasher detergent so I hopped in my car and drove to the store. On the way, a drunk driver, one of my students, ran me out of my lane and into the path of a truck. Strike one.

I ended up in a coma for weeks. My students were vigilant with cards and visits. When I woke from the coma, I was foggy and amazed by what I learned. I was told I had a brain injury. I would never run or work again. Who was there by my side along with my friends, family, and students…my MOM! Every day, she took me to physical therapy, or to the doctors. Her example of strength and perseverance through the years in dealing with her own major medical issues had shown me that with hard work and diligence I could survive. I could do the impossible. With God's grace, I did.

When I was back on my own, my parents decided it was time to make a change. All the kids were grown and creating their own adventures. Mom and Dad had decided to sell the property where we grew up in order to build a home they had designed-their dream home!

While they were building that new home, the worst possible tragedy struck. In the middle of the night, my father sat up in bed feeling strange and then fell back. The EMTs arrived within minutes and rushed him to the hospital. He never regained consciousness. My father's sudden death changed our world. Strike Two. Not only was my heart broken, but I watched my mother's world shatter. She had never been alone. They had a great life together, had survived all the ups and downs, and were never apart. The future was scary for my mom.

She found it was never too late to change your life…only death will end those choices. So the strongest woman I have ever known had to start a new phase of her life. Mom had to gather her courage in order to rebuild her life.

The home that we grew up in was very secluded. It would not have been wise for her to be isolated on the forty acres. She was unsure if she wanted to live in the new dream home either. She worked hard to finish the construction of the house while she mulled over her decision. One afternoon, we were touching up the spots the painter had missed. Determined to finish the perfect home, she climbed the ladder to touch up the paint near the roofline. Boom! Tragedy struck again as she tumbled off the ladder. As I sat by her on the ground, we looked at each other and started laughing. Everything was going to be okay. Three strikes and we were not out.

Even in death, life will always open new chapters for those that remain on Earth. The future allows us more opportunities to search for excellence and make our mark in the world. The future allows us to experience joy once again. Your future will depend on your choices.

Mom's choices allowed her to bridge her past and the future. I sold my house and moved with Mom into their treasured home. The move gave Mom the opportunity to begin her new phase of life, as my father would have wanted for her. I watched my mom become more independent as she adjusted to life without dad. She discovered that she could have fun and do things for herself. To this day, she still puts herself last while giving a thousand and ten percent to others. As she grew stronger, Mom realized new adventures were ahead.

Throughout my life, Mom has always stood by her children. Even during the craziest and most tragic times, she was there. She took on the role of mother and father, never letting us down. When I married, Mom made sure I had the perfect wedding. When I struggled, Mom was there with encouraging words. I could have never been the person I am today without her voice. I am so proud of all that my mother has achieved in life and the adventures she has experienced since my father's death. Mom was my voice that changed everything.

Dr. Carolyn Butler

Dr. Carolyn Butler is an Independent Certified Leadership Coach, Speaker and Trainer for the John Maxwell Group. She is also an Author and Organization Development Consultant. As a Leadership coach with 25 years of experience in corporate training, performance management, leadership and organizational development; she is a believer that "if there is no VISION there will be no growth". As a consultant she assists business leaders in structuring their organizational vision and mission in alignment with their desired business outcomes. She has earned a doctorate in Organizational Leadership from Northcentral University and a Master's Degree in Public Administration with a specialization in Program Development & Analysis from the University of Illinois.

Dr. Butler has a real passion for leadership effectiveness, coaching, team work facilitation and assessment feedback. In leadership development projects she applies ontological coaching methodology along with assessment instruments (360 and DISC testing). She believes in the power of a coaching relationship and helps executives, teams and companies to create long term, measurable results in leadership effectiveness. In her role as adjunct faculty for Millikin University she has taught Organizational Leadership and coached individuals from a variety of fields including sales, human resources, finance, manufacturing and small businesses.

The Vision Navigator is a Life Purpose Outreach Ministry affiliated with Love of God Ministries under the leadership of Bishop Walter Banks, Jr. Dr. Butler is the CEO and Founder of this nonprofit organization which has a mission to awaken the leader within and guide their dreams.

To learn more go to her website at http://www.thevision-navigator.com/.

Believe in Yourself

Dr. Carolyn Butler

After receiving the invitation to speak at a Christian Women's retreat on the subject of "Shaping Your Destiny", I was forced to think about my journey. My first thoughts were, "Why me; what was so great about my life?"

I had come from an abusive background where I endured many years of sexual and mental abuse. In that moment I realized that over the past twenty years I have also experienced victories. While still captured by the euphoria of the moment, my thoughts shifted to answering the question, "How did you get here?" Immediately I could hear the voice of one woman who was influential in my life say, "Believe in yourself, you are destined for greatness."

Some people come into our lives, touching every aspect of our life, and leave their thumbprint forever on our heart. Zondra was instrumental in getting me on a path that has led to this point in my life. She taught me the real meaning of self-love and perseverance amidst the many challenges that being authentic brings to your life. I didn't have a life that I could call my own;

it was all about pleasing other people in my life. Who I was and what I wanted wasn't important.

The sexual abuse by my stepfather started when I was nine years old. I grew up hating myself because I couldn't stop it from happening. Even though the sexual acts made me feel dirty on the inside and useless overall, I succumbed to them willingly. When you are sexually abused, your boundaries, your right to say no, your sense of control in the world are skewed. Rather than seeing my stepfather as a bad person, I believed instead that I was stupid and I would never succeed at anything.

Zondra came into my life at a time when I needed her the most and for that I am grateful. When things seem impossible, I hear her words echoing "You are destined for greatness, you can be whatever you want to be." She saw something inside me that I never knew existed. Courage and perseverance are the traits of her strong personality that I most prize. I have never before seen such a strong woman focus on unveiling the hidden talents and potential of others.

By the time I met Zondra I was married with two beautiful daughters. I was settled into a life that I learned to accept through my religious upbringing. Despite feelings of inadequacy I have had since childhood, my life was on track for happiness. As a devout Jehovah's Witness, you learn that if you follow all the rules, you will have a successful life. Following the rules meant acceptance, and that was important to me. My marriage was not about love, it was simply the best option for me if I wanted to have a normal life. As the wife of a man who was on track to be an Elder in the congregation, I felt a sense of my own identity.

There was a period where my family was experiencing financial hardship, and that required me to look for work outside of the home. As a Jehovah's Witness wife, it was frowned upon for me to work, unless there was a serious necessity. When I started working in the clerical pool for the organization where Ms. Zondra was the Human Resource Director, I had only one objective, and that was to work long enough to get the family out of a financial crisis.

When I met Zondra for the first time I was in awe of her presence. Here standing before me was this tall light-skinned African American woman. She had such a vibrant and boisterous spirit, and I was captivated. I witnessed firsthand that when this woman spoke, people listened. She was everything I secretly wanted to be. Yet I was there only to work in the clerical pool.

Zondra explained to me that all the job assignments were temporary throughout the organization. She made it very clear that she called people back for other assignments based solely on their performance. I wasn't worried, because I was just there on a short term basis to make some quick money, and help get the bills paid.

My first assignment was as a data entry clerk where I entered information into a computer system. During that time I would often see Zondra as she entered the cafeteria. This woman walked with authority, and in my mind she was perfect. At the end of my six week assignment I had talked with Zondra enough to form a special bond. She ignited a hidden passion in me to want more out of life.

I wasn't sure whether I measured up to her expectations. At the conclusion of that assignment I was offered another. Zondra told me that people were requesting that I come to their departments because I did such a great job. Each job assignment fed my hungering desire to be more than just a wife at home.

I never said anything to Zondra, but somehow she must have known. My six week assignment grew into two years of multiple assignments. Over the course of time, Zondra and I developed a personal friendship and I felt comfortable talking to her about the events of my life.

Zondra called me into her office during one of my assignments, just to talk. She asked me where I saw myself in the next five years. I remember telling her that my only desire was to be a good wife and mother. I talked about my religious expectations, and how they fit into my life. She gave me an odd glance, and I knew she sensed something much deeper than the answer I gave her. She followed up with a statement that touched the core of who I was at the time. She said "I don't know much about your religion, but I know you are destined for greatness and you can be more than what they conditioned you to believe."

Her next question broke the shell that had walled off my desires; "What are you afraid of?" Here was truth! I was afraid, but she had no idea of the depth of this fear. I feared that I was not going to be accepted by people if they knew my secret. I had developed a true love and respect for her, and in that moment I did not feel I measured up. With tears streaming down my face I got up and ran from her office. Zondra was in hot pursuit.

When she caught up with me, I had to make a decision. Could I trust her with this secret that had been such a major part of my life? Things can happen in anyone's life that cause you to have a different perspective. This sexual abuse in my life led me to create a new persona that transformed me into someone I could live with on a daily basis. In my mind I believed that sharing this secret with Zondra would mean that she would reject me. I ran the risk of being hated and blamed for things that happened to me, or blamed for failing to prevent them. If a secret like this was revealed, it would not only affect me and my family, but it might damage my mental state for the rest of my life.

I finally had the courage to tell Zondra what had happened to me as a child. I had been sexually abused by my stepfather, and for the longest time I was afraid, embarrassed, and ashamed to admit this to anybody. I had tried to simply forget about the traumatizing events that shaped my mindset. As a child I was introduced to sex on an adult's time table. The chance to explore life naturally, to experience my own desires for love were stolen from me. Life was distorted and I learned to disconnect myself from my emotions and my personal desires. Being silent about the abuse had just became a part of life. The feelings of unworthiness left me numb, and life was just about being successful at following the rules. My self-esteem was low, my view of love was warped, and my self-image was tarnished. I learned to shield it very well.

Once I finally shared my secret with Zondra, I waited nervously for her reaction. She reached out and grabbed my hands and looked at me with conviction and said "You are destined for greatness and you can be whatever you want to be in life." She told me that what happened to me did not change who I was, and life's circumstances do not define you as a person. Despite what I thought of myself, she told me that I was beautiful and intelligent, and that I could accomplish what I desired if I believed in myself. Zondra took on the role of mentoring me for her position. We worked together on devising a plan for me to get my college degree. With Zondra's help, I created a ten year plan that took me from a high school diploma to my doctoral degree.

About six months later, Zondra told me that she was leaving the company and moving out of state. This was devastating news for me. My heart sank with a cold feeling as I thought of the future without my mentor. As the time drew closer for her departure, I went to her, tears streaming down my face, and told her I was not sure if I would be able to carry on professionally without her. She reassured me that I had the talent and ability to do the job. I did try to live up to the professional persona that I had carved out in my mind, but the flame that she ignited me seemed to flicker out after she left the company.

It's been over twenty years since I last spoke with Zondra. We met up in Atlanta, Georgia, a few months after she settled there. She was such a significant influence in my life. I was unaware of the amazing person that was inside of me, but she saw all of the potential that I possessed.

When I was in Atlanta, I drew upon everything that Zondra taught me, and landed a job. When it came time to move to the area, I realized that I was transforming into this independent woman, destined for greatness. The only problem was that I had a husband who was not growing at the pace that I was, and I couldn't pretend that part of my life didn't exist. I married my husband with the expectation of being with him until death. As Jehovah's Witnesses, we did not believe in divorce. Changing direction meant starting over and doing it alone as a single mother of two small children.

I made the choice to defy what I was taught and pursue a life that was in alignment with the desires that had been trapped inside of me. I wanted a career, and even though I wasn't clear as to what that would be, I knew I needed a college degree. My direct support in the decision to go back to school came from Zondra. I did eventually file for divorce, and the struggles of being a single parent working and going to school were not easy.

Still, I made it. Both of my daughters have completed college and have successful careers of their own.

Recently I came across a card that Zondra had sent me. Once again I received this at a time when I needed to be encouraged to stay the course. It was if she knew I had started doubting myself again. These are the last words that I received from my mentor in a card entitled "Believe in Yourself". Inside the card were these words: "Doubt whom you will but never yourself".

Zondra wrote: "Dearest Carolyn, I saw this card and I just knew you would like it. Just as the card states, you have every-thing it takes to make an impact on the world. You are definitely destined for greatness, and you have to believe that about your-self. People see your strength and it can be intimidating, but you have to continue to be you. Many await the unveiling of your gift because many will benefit. However, that potential—the gift that you have inside of you—will remain dormant unless you start believing in yourself. Your circumstance doesn't define who are you or who you can be. Use those incidents of the past and future to harness more power from within. Love Z."

It has taken a lifetime to get comfortable with the person God created me to be. I take pride in having known such a powerful woman. As the saying goes, sometimes people come into your life only for a season. Reflecting on the timing of my meeting Zondra, I know she was meant to be there at that time in my life. She served a particular purpose in my life that let me see who I could become. She was the voice that made a difference in my life then, and she continues to have a profound effect on who I am today.

There are some valuable lessons I learned from Zondra. I learned how to endure tragedies and build strength. When horrible things happen, the pain is real, and these events are obstacles to moving ahead with your life. Within the soul lies the strength to move any and all obstacles that are in your way. Zondra taught me to always "focus on the finish line". She taught me how, with confidence, I can achieve anything I set my mind to. It took many years to understand the essence of who I am today. Equipped with the knowledge and the words of wisdom from my mentor, I made some life changing decisions. At the beginning of January, 2015; I decided to define the life that I wanted to live and began the journey to accomplish all that my heart desires.

If Zondra could see me now. Her words of encouragement still linger as I challenge myself with new opportunities that require me to step out of my comfort zone. I miss my mentor tremendously, and I don't know where she is today. I miss her strength, her passion for life and the moments we shared. I accomplished the goal we set together. I received my doctoral degree and now I am moving to Atlanta to live my dream. What is my dream? My ultimate goal is to be an Evangelist who travels and speak throughout the world. That desire unleashed another hidden passion that I had put aside for many years—that is writing. It was something I just stopped doing because it did not fit into the life that I had originally carved out for myself.

Today I am in a very good place, I love myself—I love my life and love where I am headed. I am open to learning and experiencing new adventures. I now have the confidence that I once saw in Zondra; I don't ignore things I want for myself, and I have learned to let go of people who don't support my dreams. Most importantly, I believe in me. Everyone should have a person they consider to be their mentor. These people influence you and the decisions you make. They are the Voice that Changed Everything. I can honestly say that I might never have taken this step if it weren't for Zondra's support and confidence in me.

Thank you Zondra for believing in me and helping me to believe in myself.

Karin Rowlee Kincaid

My husband and I have been together for over 18 years. We have 2 beautiful children, a boy and a girl, as well as, a little voiced cat, named Tokyo. I was born and raised in the foothills of southeast Tennessee where I spent many of my days playing in the woods, climbing trees, and dancing. During my early teenage years, I experienced a life altering illness which naturally turned into an interest in the healing arts. Before heading to college, I nurtured my spirit further and took the opportunity to develop my self-confidence working as a raft guide on the Ocoee River in TN for over 10 years, as well as, working on the New and Gauley Rivers in West Virginia.

Initially I attended college at Cleveland State Community College where my father taught Chemistry, later transferring to UGA where I attained a BA in Anthropology in 2002 and a Minor in Chinese Language & Literature studying abroad in China for one summer. I attended the Atlanta School of Massage where I became certified in

Clinical Massage and Neuromuscular Therapies, then opened a small business, Gwinnett Muscular Pain Center where I worked as a massage therapist for many years. I currently reside in Metro Atlanta as a work-from-home mom. My passion is helping others learn how to feed their body for healing from and prevention of disease as well as mentoring others in changing lifestyles.

Contacts: #theRecoveringIntrovert, @krowlee on Twitter, and Karin Rowlee Kincaid on Facebook. karin4jp@gmail.com

Karin's Voice

The Story of Dad: A Father's Gift

Karin Rowlee Kincaid

My father was an eccentric man. Not eccentric in a collector of fine worldly artifacts, or marvelously and culturally rare things kind-of-way, but eccentric, as in a socially awkward, hoarder of old computer parts, unwanted papers, broken things and model trains kind-of-way. Even as a young child I recognized that my dad just didn't see things quite the same way that my friends' parents did.

I first noticed this eccentricity in his choice for leisure activity. On any given Sunday, he would pack us (my mom, my two older brothers and me) up in the car following Sunday school and spend the whole day chasing trains and just generally losing track of time, and any knowledge of where we were on a map. Only after finding ourselves in yet another new location after yet another train faded from view, would we finally stop to eat at a local dive—normally somewhere in the midst of the Appalachian mountains.

He had a great sense of direction, however, and part of the fun was trying to navigate our way back from where we had been. This was also beneficial for learning purposes, as it taught me how to orient myself and read a map. We would return home so late at night that the three of us children would be sound asleep in the back of our 1970's blue and white striped van, and had to be carried into bed.

Then it was time to go on a trans-American summer long road trip. Instead of renting a U-haul or some other pre-made trailer to tote our things, he designed a DIY "luggage box" made of plywood which sat at the far end of a 20ft long boat trailer. Now, you might say that it was an extremely resourceful thing to do (and no doubt it was), but the "box" sat so far back toward the rear of the trailer that we forgot it was behind us; we were constantly plagued by the feeling that something creepy was following us. I'm sure there were many UFO sightings reported to the local authorities along our journey since, to the observers along the roadside, the box hovering before them had nothing to do with the red station wagon that had just passed. Regardless of what memory I recall, there is no doubt that he was one of a kind!

His inherent nature was only enhanced by his chosen profession. He was a chemistry professor at the local community college—the quintessential mad scientist, if you will. He was loved by many of his former students, and his unique and unusual perspective on life was always appreciated (in a humorous kind of way) by many of the faculty and staff. It was not unusual to find him sitting in his office grading papers, unaware of the time, pleasantly whistling whatever tune sprung forth from his mind.

Students, faculty, and staff would frequently stop by to have a quick chat with my father throughout the day, as he was a dedicated and permanent fixture at the college for over 42 years. Of course, one had to be cautious of the mounds of student papers and lab books stacked ceiling high. To this day, most people fondly remember the half tucked in shirts, ink spotted shirt pockets (later corrected by pocket protectors), hand ruffled hair, dry sense of humor, quirky, and compassionate man that was my father. Exemplifying their love and appreciation of him, a class once gave him a wooden paddle as a year end gift. On one side of the paddle was written the name "Mr. Molecule," followed on the opposite side by the phrase "Old chemists never die, they just simply fail to react."

His personal organization system (or complete lack thereof) highlighted yet another extension of his idiosyncratic personality. It appeared to be a system based on his inability to throw anything away. This system was closely tied both to different eras of his professional and personal life, as well as the functional use of space. Once he ran out of horizontal space in a room, he would then coordinate vertically, beginning with his most recent work until it was too high for him to access. My father was a tall man so for anyone trying to assist him in retrieving an item, it was most unfortunate.

Eventually, the vertical ascent of papers and manuals would begin again in a new location. Though items were all chronologically placed, they weren't nicely organized into files. In his unconventional thinking, piles functioned well enough as a readily accessible and easily understood system, so they should be easily understood by others as well. However, his lab assistant, bless her heart, once or twice attempted, and failed, to bring a sense of tidiness and sanity to his office. But no matter, it was the same at home.

My mother recently stated that one of the ways in which my father showed his love for a person was to spend time doing things with and for them. As children, my brothers and I shared many special moments with him: playing "tickle monster," riding to school and back, and making special outings and trips during the summers. I remember many moments of joyous laughter listening to his rolling chuckle. It was the kind of laugh that made everyone else around him laugh even more.

On one occasion, I went to watch a movie at the local theater with my father. Inadvertently, all attention was drawn to us when his laughter well outlasted the funny scene in the film that had caused it in the first place. The cycle of laughter for everyone else had long since ended, however, as his infectious laughter continued, it began to take hold of everyone in that audience. Within a few moments, the whole theater was cackling and not one person could resist. I quickly overcame my brief moment of embarrassment as I recognized that the ability to command a whole room, just by laughing, was a fairly remarkable skill. It truly was a unique laugh!

As my brothers and I grew older, it became more and more difficult for him to share his love with us through the sharing of his time. As teenagers, we naturally began to find interests and activities of our own. Additionally, in his abstract and emotionally voiceless mind, communication simply was used as a means of conveying practical information, not necessarily a way to express uncomfortable and fleeting emotions. As a result, none of us received adequate amounts of time, attention, direction, or physical nurturing. In my development, this deficit caused me to be shy, timid, and introverted. There was a sense that I too had the inability to express my feelings or embrace my uninhibited potential.

Don't get me wrong, he was a brilliant man who was able to do many things well. He was also a good friend to many people—providing instruction not only in the world of chemistry, but in many other basic concepts of life. However, his inability to verbally express his love was evident. It wasn't until he realized that he might not be here for as long as he had originally planned that he began to say things out loud and without hesitation.

I vividly remember one such moment during his last few weeks of his life. I was sitting next to him on the couch and he said outright, with no beginning or end, "I love you." It was a pattern, as I learned that during his first hospitalization, there was just such a moment between he and my mother as well. The exchange between them, through tears of forgiveness and with just a minimum of words spoken, rectified the disappointments and resentments of unspoken emotion shared during their 43 year marriage. Then, there were even more words of sadness as he realized he would not have the opportunity to be "a good Grandpop" to my son.

I was not always confident in who I thought my father was. The years I spent chasing my own life and not knowing what kept his time occupied, left me feeling that I did not know him very well at all. Neither one of us made it a priority to connect often enough. Yet, there was always something in my core being that told me he was the type of man that would give someone the shirt off of his back or do all that he could to help someone in need. I never doubted that he loved me. Still, because there was no literal voice affirming my thoughts about who he was, there was doubt about his character. This doubt persisted right up until the day of his memorial service.

I spent the weeks prior to the service meticulously combing through old photographic slides of our family. I thought I had seen most of our photos, however, I came across some that were taken before the arrival of my brothers and me into the family. There were pictures of my mother and father as a young couple and, thanks to his sister, even some of my father as a young child. I began having conversations with my mother about their earlier years together and other meaningful moments.

We spoke of simple but very special moments between them while they were dating, and in their early years of marriage. From the outside, it might have looked as though my father was, in his detached way, simply going through obligatory motions of courtship (or marriage). There were flowers given prior to a formal banquet, cherries shared between the two, and vacation plans that changed at the last minute. But there is more significance to these examples if we take a closer look.

The flowers he bought for the banquet were orchids. During the 1960's, purchasing orchids in the middle of the US would not have been easy, or inexpensive. Unlike today, where purchasing any variety of flower and having it delivered is a mouse click away, back then it was no easy matter. They had to be ordered through a florist in Iowa, who then called a supplier in Hawaii, who finally shipped the flowers back to Iowa. Likewise, cherries were an uncommon and expensive commodity at that time in the mid-west, and required similar effort to obtain.

My mom was the daughter of a preacher, which did not lend itself to many instances of expensive foods. Upon hearing that she loved cherries, he surprised her with a box of them, to be enjoyed on a boat excursion down the Chicago River. This, I realized, is what my mother meant when she said he showed his love to someone by doing things with and for them.

My mother was diagnosed with Fibromyalgia in the late 1980's. After struggling with this chronic and oppressive condition for some time, she had the notion that sitting on a beach somewhere might be helpful in lifting her spirits. She mentioned it offhandedly to my father. She hadn't realized that my father had already made plans to go on a trip to visit a friend. However, she overheard a phone conversation shortly thereafter in which he was explaining to someone that his wife never asked for much, so he wanted "to do this for her." Before she knew it they were sitting on the beach at Tybee Island.

This and other stories continued at his memorial service; I was overwhelmed by the outpouring of gratitude.

One story was told by a young lady who was planning to drop out of college. She was having difficulty attending classes because she was caring for an infant child. She had quite a few tests to make up, and therefore, she felt that her education was a lost cause. My father, being the practical man he was, couldn't imagine that this alone would be enough to force someone to drop out. So, as she came in to take these tests, he held and cared for her baby.

Another story was told by a disabled young man. Although he was in a wheelchair, he fought quite fiercely for his independence. On one occasion, my father accompanied him to a Christian music festival. They encountered many obstacles, during which my father always offered his assistance. The young man politely but firmly refused each consecutive offer of help—in getting out of the car, or navigating the rows of bleachers in an outdoor stadium. Then came the stinging heavy rain; only then was the offer of help hastily accepted. The young man attempted to hold the umbrella over both of them while my father traversed the uneven terrain and puddles as he pushed the wheelchair to the car. Ultimately, they both thought it was a most humorous moment.

As the stories continued, I learned that my father was the kind of man who would go out of his way to care for someone. It was a deeply ingrained aspect of who he was, forged in the heart of a post depression era Midwest and rooted largely in his religious upbringing. His actions were not void of joy; rather, every moment was a curious observation of life, humanity, dignity, and the opportunity for humor. He never expected anything in return- no reward or recognition. In his mind, it was just what you did. Most certainly, it was not done to be boastful, prideful, or braggadocios.

It was just as much a matter of practicality as it was a matter of doing what was right. He never talked about what he was doing when he helped people. As a matter of fact, most of what I learned about my father's good deeds were not disclosed to me at all until people began sharing their stories at his memorial service. He truly cared for those around him, and considered almost anyone to be a friend no matter their circumstance. In this way, my father made the biggest impact on me he could have ever made. I got to see a legacy of kindness carried out by a person with a true servant's heart.

Without him being fully aware of his impact, he consistently sought out the opportunity to bring a little joy into someone's life, or to help ease their burdens. He was so fully immersed in those moments that time had no meaning or hold on his choices. Consequently, his inability to reconcile time brought a little sadness and disappointment to my own life. On several occasions, I had to walk a couple of miles to his work because he had forgotten to pick me up from school. Despite this lapse in his own judgement, my father's selfless gift of his time with others ultimately far outweighed any undesirable effects experienced in my own life.

It is the small acts of kindness he demonstrated throughout his life that now assure me of who he was. Had I the emotional knowledge or confidence to ask, he would have done anything for me. It was never an issue of him not wanting to connect with me; he just didn't know how to connect emotionally. It was much easier for him to connect with me by taking action rather than by talking. In this way, he was always there for me.

In his lifetime of actions, I recognized my father's faith in Christ. I saw that the most important relationship of all is the one he had with his Heavenly Father. I learned that Christ is the one who teaches us how to treat other people and, despite our deficiencies, He is the one that forgives us when we fail in those same relationships. Up to that point (36 years of my life), I was unsure of who Christ was to me.

In a sense, my father's life was a symbolic representation of my relationship with Christ. No matter what emotional distance I perceived in my relationship with my father, he completely surrendered his life to serving others. All along, he was waiting on the sidelines to do the same for me, if only I had asked. He had always been on my side and it is precisely through my father's actions that I came to know that Christ operates in the same manner.

I don't know why my father died when he did, but to me it felt like he died so that I could see the wholeness of his person. I could appreciate his strengths and forgive his weakness. In his absence, I clung to my own personal relationship with Christ where my sins could be forgiven, and through Him I could live the life of service that He would have me live.

So, I will affirm to you the old adage, actions do speak louder than words. While there will always be regrets of not fully understanding who my father was while he was alive or being able to adequately communicate with him about it, I thank God that my father was able to show through his actions what is truly important in life. It was a gift that has forever changed my life.

The Voice That Changed Everything for me was not an audible one, yet it's impact was as loud and clear as if had been spoken. Each of us have but a brief moment in time and history to make an impact in others' lives…to leave a legacy of sorts. While it is always important to improve ourselves, it has never been solely for the purpose of seeing what we can accomplish individually. It has always been about the opportunity to impact the lives of others in powerful and meaningful ways—to make the world an awesome and wondrous place to live—not just for ourselves, but for generations to come. And with God's tender grace guiding the way, I truly believe we can do so.

My father had just retired from 42 years of teaching and was still tutoring students in chemistry when he was afflicted with the rare disease known as Creutzfeldt-Jakob Disease (CJD). The disease process was as eccentric and uncommon as my father; only one in a million are afflicted by it. The time from the onset of his awareness of his symptoms to the time of his death was just over four weeks. We had four weeks to watch my father stay as strong in his intellect as his impaired memory allowed, yet experience what it looked like for the disease to move through his brain and, consequently, affect the different areas of his body.

There are no specific tests that diagnose CJD while the patient is living. It is only when testing for other possible diseases comes back negative that CJD begins to emerge as a culprit. A final diagnosis is given through postmortem brain biopsy. I greatly appreciate the efforts of the CJD Foundation in their commitment in educating the medical community, hospice workers, and funeral home directors, as well as, their support for CJD families.

For more information regarding CJD or to donate to the CJD Foundation in memorandum of my father, Ed Rowlee, go to https://www.cjdfoundation.org

If you'd like to contribute to the legacy of caring that was embodied by my father, please consider donating to the Ed Rowlee Memorial Scholarship Fund at Cleveland State Community College, Cleveland TN. Contact Barbara Eaves, secretary at the CSCC Foundation office. (423) 472-7141.

Diane Freeman

Diane is a personal stylist and a leading expert in boosting women's self-confidence. Specializing in women over 40, Diane has 15 years of experience as a serial entrepreneur representing makeup, skincare, jewelry and most recently, patented confidence-boosting clothing. Diane has coached hundreds of women and has thoroughly enjoyed seeing her clients bloom. Diane's coaching helps women to make their best choice for superior health, image, finances and self-confidence.

Diane is also passionate about building self-esteem in tween and teen girls. She has volunteered thousands of hours to help girls get involved in sports with a special love for the lifetime sport of swimming. She has volunteered hundreds of hours leading "self esteem, inner beauty" birthday parties for girls. She also supports women entrepreneurs via her networking and speaking.

Diane Freeman offers personal styling appointments in person in the Atlanta area and virtually throughout the US. She is also seeking dynamic women who wish to join her team. Her Ruby Ribbon team of "Dreamweavers" boosts the self-confidence of women throughout the US and teaches women to support others while at the same time building her own personal vision.

Diane has a recognized blog www.charmedbydiane.com where she would love to hear your feedback. You may also contact her via her clothing website www.rubyribbon.com/dianefreeman or via email at Diane@charmedbydiane.com

The Voices of Many Mothers

Diane Freeman

When I was four years old, sitting on my dad's lap, I once again asked him the dreaded question. "Daddy, when is Mommy coming home?"

It was the third time I had asked that question in two days. Either I could not comprehend the answer, or I hoped that if I prayed hard enough the answer would change. The answer was the same. "Mommy is in Heaven with God and she is not coming home." At that moment, I finally realized my mother was gone.

My mother had struggled with a congenital heart defect, so as soon as I could walk and understand instructions, I was her big helper. I learned early to climb into my highchair when my mother could not lift me, and I helped with household chores. I could even toddle into McDonald's and order and pay for my food, and order her hamburger with "no salt" while she waited for me in the car. Too weak to do it herself, I climbed upon the "big bed" to turn on the tall oxygen tanks when my mother had trouble breathing.

I probably saved my mother's life several times at the young age of three, but her heart was just too weak to continue living any longer. My mother, Mary Ann Pellino Flathers, passed away when she was only 30 years old. My last memory was watching as the EMTs wheeled her out of my grandmother's house on a stretcher. Because my mother did not want me to see her in the hospital, and my family thought it best that I not attend the funeral, I never saw her again.

I was the only child of a sick only child, so out of necessity my mother taught me that I could take care of myself and others. She was the first person to see my greatness and help me develop it. It is amazing the things I still remember learning from her, even though I was so young. Hers was definitely the first voice to contribute to my greatness.

Even in her death, I learned from my mother. I learned that important people get called up to Heaven, and we should appreciate them while they are here. I also learned that if I could get over *that* painful hurdle, of loss and loneliness, then I could get over anything. I could have been angry with God, but instead I chose to follow Him because He showed His face to me by comforting and supporting me my entire life. God helped through that time of loss, but I didn't realize that a secret awaited me, one that would forever change my view of myself and where I came from.

In the 1970's, daycare did not exist in our small town in Connecticut, but my father's job required international travel. So, when my mother died, I went to live with my aunt and uncle. My aunt was a stay-at-home mom who was kind and nurturing.

My Uncle Rich and Aunt Carol took me into their family and made me feel I was a part of it. They lived about an hour away from my father, and for five years I only saw him on weekends, when he was not traveling.

During this five-year period, Aunt Carol was my mother figure. She made sure I had everything I needed. She played the role of my mother at school and kept me connected with my grandparents and cousins. Both my Aunt Carol and Uncle Rich taught me that family is who you accept, and I appreciate all they did for me. They made me feel important and helped me learn that love, not just blood, makes a family.

My father remarried when I was nine. After he returned to his home with my "new mother," I went to live with them. Betty, my stepmother, married my father with plans of having her own family. In fact, she was pregnant on her wedding day, and I was beyond thrilled to be living with my father, my new mother and future siblings.

Although I lived in her house, I never felt like I was Betty's child. I had high expectations of my new mother, expectations that she could not fulfill. Because my mother was gone, my child's mind assumed Betty would take on the role. I expected her to be like the mothers on TV, but Betty's personality was not at all like Carol Brady or June Cleaver. For many years, I thought she was mean when she denied me sugary snacks or made me do household chores or my own laundry, even though she washed everyone else's clothes.

I felt Betty cared less for me than the other children. So, during my teen years in particular, I rebelled against everything she did, and even considered running away. I am thankful that, somehow, I had enough common sense to keep me from doing anything *that* dumb. Although I would never be "her" child, Betty still treated me respectfully, and her insistence on holding me accountable for chores and laundry taught me the lesson of self-reliance.

Thank you, Betty, for adding to the voices of the mothers in my life, for raising me along with your children, and for helping me to live with my father. Had you not raised me from nine years old to eighteen, I would not be the person I am today.

When I was sixteen years old, I found out through a relative's slip of the tongue that I was adopted. The news rocked my world. HARD!! I was very clueless about my adoption. So clueless that I failed my own blood test! Earlier, in my biology class, we were learning about dominant and recessive traits, including hair and eye color, the ability to curl the tongue, and blood types. The semester ended with our teacher determining our blood type through an in-class test. I believed I was a genetic miracle. I had fair skin, blonde hair and green eyes and my blood type is AB negative. My parents both had dark brown hair, dark brown eyes and olive skin. They also both had O positive blood. I searched my family tree down three generations trying to justify my findings. Despite that rather clear evidence, I was shocked to learn the news of my adoption.

At first I was really angry with my father and stepmother for keeping this crucial information from me. I felt like my family, neighbors, and friends knew a huge secret that I did not. Like many adopted children, I immediately questioned who I was. Everything I thought I knew about myself—my genetic background, cultural background, inherited personality traits—was a lie. My adoptive parents were of Italian and Polish descent and were the first generation born here from parents who immigrated to the states. Much of my lifestyle focused on the traditions of both Polish and Italian people. We ate ethnic foods, occasionally attended Catholic church in Italian or Polish and I even picked up on the occasional Italian or Polish curse word as my grandparents each spoke their native language. It was a huge part of my identity. I had just finished an English project where I wrote an autobiography, and I focused on being brought up in two different ethnic homes. When I learned I was adopted I felt that whole story was false.

I continued to feel lost for several months. I took great interest in every woman above the age of 30 with light hair and eyes, wondering if she could be my birth mother . I even wondered if a well-liked teacher could have been my mother as we had some similar features and she was the right age.

I was so afraid my friends and family would treat me differently once the secret was out that I was not genetically related to my family. I was sure they would cut me off, and that they would never treat me like a blood relative again. However, my family and friends did just the opposite! They made me feel more loved than ever. It was heartwarming to hear them tease me about all of the silly family traits I would not have, and to point out the ones I seemed to have inherited anyway, such as skinny legs and a big butt. My family saw me as important, and reminded me once again that love is stronger than blood.

When I turned 18, I went off to college, as many young adults do. It was a great period of growth in my life. I was a focused student and got involved on campus, but I never could put to rest the nagging thought that my mother was out there in the world somewhere.

I met my future husband freshman year. We dated for six years and got married just a few months after he completed his MBA.

We had a great time in our early 20s, traveling the country with our jobs, and enjoying every moment of being young newlyweds.

After five years of marriage, we found ourselves in our first home, and pregnant with our first child. We were overjoyed! I had an easy pregnancy, but the medical forms were difficult when I could not answer any questions about my family's medical history. By the end of my pregnancy, I had begun the journey to discover the "non-identifying" information about my parents, which was quite a process! I petitioned the court several times to have my records opened, but the judge refused. I was going to have to find other ways to learn about my medical background.

I still remember being in the hospital room the evening after my first beautiful child, a girl, was born. While holding her in the rocking chair, I gazed in to her angelic blue eyes. I thought to myself, "Imagine if I did not get to keep her. What if I had to give her away?"

Tears came to my eyes at the thought. It was at this moment that I decided I needed to find my birth mother. I had to know what kind of person had the strength I knew it must have taken to give her child up for adoption.

I already knew some things about her, as bits of information had been revealed about my parents through my adoption documents.

It took three years of petitioning the courts, and hiring a private investigator, to get the information I truly wanted—the name of my birth mother, Carolyn Foulds. I finally had it! Now, it was up to me to contact her and let her know I wanted to meet her. This was a scary, yet exhilarating thought.

The private investigator suggested that I call my maternal grandmother and pretend I was with a school reunion committee, and that I needed to contact Carolyn to invite her to the next reunion. Fortunately, Edith Foulds, my maternal grandmother, answered the phone and gave me the information that I needed. She also gave me the married name, address and phone number of my MOTHER!

It took several letters, and months of planning, before I was able to meet my mom, Carolyn (Lyn) Brown. She was in her third marriage, and her husband did not know she had ever had a child. Therefore, she had to be creative and plan it just right, as she was not ready to tell him.

Lyn and I met at Logan airport in Boston, Massachusetts, the city of my birth. It seemed the most sensible place to meet, given that I lived in Florida and she lived in Canada. We spent the whole day together in Boston, where I learned a lot about both of us. I learned that not only was I her only child, I was also the only child of her entire family. Neither my mother's sister (coincidentally named Diane, just like me) nor her brother ever had any children. This, of course, meant that my grandparents had no grandchildren, and there were no prospects of any.

I learned that Lyn was a social worker when she got pregnant with me. She'd had a bit too much to drink one evening, and was feeling sad over a breakup, when she had unprotected sex with my father. She learned a month later she was pregnant, and never told my biological father.

She did tell her parents, though, and her father forced her to leave home. Lyn's father was a prominent leader in his religious community, and he was embarrassed to have a pregnant, unwed daughter. He told the entire family to disown her.

Lyn, being a social worker, knew firsthand the difficulty of raising a child alone in 1966 and thought it was best to give me a better future by putting me up for adoption. She left her home in Vermont and went to live in a shelter for unwed mothers in Boston. My grandmother managed to sneak away from her husband to see me in the hospital before I was taken away. She knew it was her one chance to see her only grandchild.

Meeting my birth mother made me even more grateful for my adoptive mother, my aunt and my stepmother. I understand the sacrifice that my birth mother and all my "mother figures" made. But, Lyn's sacrifice was especially touching since she had no other children. Lyn Brown and I are still in touch. She even attended my 18-year-old daughter's high school graduation, and has visited us during the summer. She is grateful for the opportunity to get to know her only child and grandchildren, and I am happy to know her.

I feel extra lucky to have known my birth mother's mother, Edith Foulds. I really got to know Edith after my other three grandmothers passed away. (I had three mothers between my mother Mary Ann, Aunt Carol, and Betty, so I had three grandmothers as well.) The opportunity to have another grandmother after I had lost the others was a great blessing.

Edith was a model grandmother. She had been a teacher in her younger years, and was delighted to raise her three children in rural Vermont. She was an excellent cook, teacher, writer, seamstress and more. She also exuded love. Edith experienced great joy in meeting me and my husband, but she was especially joyous when she met her great grandchildren. She was able to meet my daughter at age three, and my son when he was one. She so lovingly made the long trip from Vermont to Florida to visit us, even when she was in poor health.

Edith wrote us beautiful handwritten letters with excellent penmanship, despite her poor eyesight. She told all of us constantly how thrilled she was to know us, and I think when her life came to an end at 93; she felt it was much better lived because she knew our generation would carry on.

I am grateful to Edith for being a role model parent and grandparent, even though she did not get to be a grandparent until later in life. I believe that is why she was so good at it; she appreciated the chance to know her family while so many of us take it for granted. The best part is that Edith's loving voice will be passed down for many generations to come, thanks to a book that she contributed to, which recorded our family's history.

Finally, I must recognize my husband's mother. Throughout all of the busy times of raising children and digging up new relatives, my mother-in-law, Peggy Freeman, cheered me on. She made phone calls for me, and helped me discover my birth mother's name. She babysat while I left to meet Lyn, and helped out many other times, even when it meant she had to travel quite a distance. She has been an outstanding mother to both me and her son and daughter, and an exceptional grandmother, accepting me as her daughter from the moment I married her son.

The voices of the mothers in my life have all contributed to shaping me and making me who I am today. Some were related to me by birth; others, by marriage or by adoption. But there is one thing they all have in common: Their voices gave me my own voice, and helped me find my greatness. I will always be truly thankful for the things I gained from each and every one of my many mothers.

Bernadette,

You inspire me every
day! Thank you!!!

Love,
Shelly

Shelly Steele

Shelly Steele, known in recent years as a 'Voice of Steele', has been a catalyst for growth and development for companies, products and brands most of her career life. She is now the successful owner of her own company, Shelly Steele Voice Talent, providing on and off stage acting and training.

Years of training and experience have resulted in a proven track record of excellence. Application of her speaking and business skills to the world of Voice Acting was a perfect fit, and she loves what she does.

Her desire is to help companies and organizations effectively communicate their objectives, and she has already demonstrated  this by successfully supporting a large variety of genres, both in corporate and small business settings. Her greatest strengths in business have been project management, team and personal leadership, insight, business development and customized client solutions. Toastmasters International uncovered her love of speaking and training, and ultimately led to acting and voice acting.

A primary focus on English and communication during her college years was an additional foundation for her future. She has received extensive training from many top voice talents, actors, managers, and technicians from around the globe. Character development and script analysis are key in her industry. She now proudly portrays a great number of characters and inspirations with her voice. She has volunteered and read for The Fulton County Library System programs, Recipe for Hope, various nationwide schools, Association of Information Technology Professionals, and a 77 year old Charter Atlanta Garden Club, Livestrong and Enable of Georgia. Personal character traits many use to describe Shelly include encouraging, creative, tenacious, thoughtful, placing faith and family first, a strong work ethic, a visionary, friendly, compassionate, bold, and hospitable.

Home has been various locations throughout the U.S., but is now Roswell, Georgia, USA. Her immediate family resides in Georgia as well.

Contact Shelly:
shelly@shellysteelevoicetalent.com
www.shellysteelevoicetalent.com
Twitter: shellysteele1
www.shellysteele/facebook.com

Shelly's Voice

One of These Days

Shelly Steele

A ll we really have is now. A kind soul, Nita, reminded me of that.

When most people reflect on their life, they realize there was a particular someone who had an unusual impact on them. For me, there are too many to list in one chapter, but it was requested that I choose just one.

Nita Sanders, 86, a dear family friend, said something to me recently that turned my life upside down. Many have said or done things that have impacted me greatly, but she shared something profound that changed everything for me at this juncture in my life, and I decided that she fit the description of "the voice that changed everything".

I attended a life celebration memorial for a friend Matt's father when Nita spoke to me. Two weeks prior to that, I had been at the same church saying good-bye to my father-in-law, who passed away following a short bout with bladder cancer. I was deep in thought about how life begins, how we navigate through it the best way we can, and how it ends. It is fleeting, and goes by fast.

As I was pondering these thoughts, Nita approached me. She said she missed my mother-in-law who had passed away four years ago, and thanked me for being thoughtful, kind, and staying in touch. Her dear Sam had just passed away a few months earlier, after a lifetime of love. I asked her if I could treat her to a nice lunch soon. She smiled and said "Yes, we will have to do that one of these days". I stopped breathing for what felt like a minute…for me…that was life changing. I had barely slept in days, and was working long hours, accompanied by travel and many other obligations. The next couple of days, those words ran through my mind. How could I get off the treadmill I suddenly felt I was on, and start taking the time I have left more seriously? The contrast of looking at memorial pictures of this man's lifetime at the memorial that day, and her words "one of these days" felt like a bright spotlight and woke me up. What if there isn't enough time for projecting "one of these days" events? What if our best intentions never make it off the to-do list? I've often heard people say they hope their dreams don't die with them. I know I don't want that to happen to me.

I thought of the many people I had known in my lifetime who had passed on, moved away or became former colleagues. I still felt them in my mind, and in my heart. I thought there would always be more time. More time!

My last visit with my father-in-law on Father's Day; a few days before he died, flashed in my mind. My friend and colleague who thought he would be dancing with his daughter at her wedding, passed away three weeks before the big day. My sister-in-law and many friends have been given a diagnosis of cancer, and they strive to overcome and heal, some succeed and some don't. So many of us believe we have all the time in the world. "Stop the

Treadmill and Live." I thought. Nita's words stirred me, and I realized that "one of these days" often translates to <u>maybe soon, or never or too late,</u> and I refused to accept that anymore. Life is too valuable, and people are too precious to let it go so easily.

I reached out to Nita after that, and asked her to join me for lunch the following week instead of "one of these days".

Something else made it even more special. My granddaughter Brooke joined us. We tried on vintage hats and gloves, and had a delightful ladies tea and luncheon at local shop called Tea Leaves & Thyme. Brooke was going back to school the next day. It was an ideal way to end her summer vacation, and she loved that shop. Nita was happy to share our lunch date, and they just adored each other.

Over the years, I noticed that one of Brooke's favorite sayings when she has another fun and adventurous day is "This was the best day of my life!" We <u>all</u> loved it! It made me hungry for more of them.

When I was her age, I was also full of love and adventure, and gratitude. I have never taken those early years of my life for granted. I was blessed with loving parents, grandparents, extended family, an older sister and brother, two twin brothers, friends, and a beautiful home in a small town in Iowa. Prior to that, my parents completed college in Michigan, married, and then relocated to Iowa where dad finished his medical residency. He accepted a position as partner at the medical office in town, and I'm told the community loved him. He saw patients during the day, and outside the office he delivered babies and aided those in need of medical care some nights and week-ends.

He was able to save my life when I was about two years old. I became very ill, and almost died of complications due to pneumonia. I'm sure it was a very frightening time for my family; especially with baby twins and two older siblings to care for at the same time. Neighbors and friends helped a lot. I had more to accomplish in life I suppose because I recovered fully.

Sadly, recovery wasn't possible for dad. His compromised heart was weakened, and after a series of tests, and trip to the Mayo Clinic in Rochester, we learned that his time was running out after a brief 31 years of life. He took a trip to Colorado, against his physician's advice, but it was his last wish. He then spent the remainder of his time with his family until his death in April.

I don't remember any of this, but our faith in God, family and friends helped us through it all. That was the first time I experienced a broken heart. Mom said they couldn't get me to stop crying. They called a priest, and I guess it helped, but no one knows what he said to me. That was probably the first voice that changed everything, even though I will never know what he said.

I believe that our priest, family, friends, and community instilled influences in me that I have passed along to others in my life. I am often told I am thoughtful, compassionate, kind and caring. Their actions were my first lesson in the importance of those virtues.

Mom and dad likely thought they had many years ahead of them, and that "one of these days" they would make more time to rest and enjoy life again. As experience makes clear, we can't know the time or the hour.

I witnessed and learned from the strength and courage of my family, then and now. Referring often to the bible's Chapter of 1 Corinthians, I often prayed for the wisdom to apply those lessons of love in my daily life. Often I skipped lunch in elementary school during Lent so I could walk to the nearby church and pray for that guidance. I felt very safe there. No matter what else changed, I felt I could turn to God.

My youth sheltered me from many of the challenges the family faced in the next few years. I kept busy with tap and ballet dancing, piano, camps, the annual rodeo and other small town activities and traditions. My favorite childhood memories are the trips we took to the lakes in Iowa, Wisconsin and Michigan. The Wisconsin Dells, Warren Dunes of Michigan, and my fun with relatives provided many happy memories! Mom fell in love again, and married a man we also loved greatly. We affectionately began calling him our Daddy John. He was, and always has been, a precious gift to us. After some time they had a child, my sweet brother Marty!

Not long after that, a few years after their marriage, Daddy John took up a new career, and we moved to Ankeny, a suburb of Des Moines, Iowa. It was a good move for the family, but it was so hard to leave our home, my best friend Jeanie, and the security of small town life.

There were more changes to come. My sister went off to college, and my close relationship with my older brother dimmed a bit with his newfound interest in cars, sports, girls and new friends. It was at that time, just a few short months after our move, that a tornado destroyed a large portion of our home. We were all away on some errands, and my older brother was alone at home working on his car. As the storm escalated, he ran to the house. As he stepped inside the door on the stairwell, a roof from another house slammed into the back of our house, knocking him down the stairs. He realized that broken glass from a shattered window was peppered in his eyes. He could not close them, and had to prop open his eye lids with his fingers. He then sought refuge under a desk and waited until help arrived. We found Bill, and were relieved to find that he only had minor injuries! When we drove up to see the house after the storm, I was in shock, but I will never forget how calm and collected Daddy John was. He taught me a great lesson that day about facing adversity with courage and a clear mind; to take whatever action was needed.

We had to live in the basement, and bring in water and food and begin repairs. Neighbors rallied to help one another, and eventually things returned to some sense of normalcy, along with a big helping of gratitude.

Soon enough I was in high school. I stayed very busy. Some of my activities included honor society and cheerleading, and I developed a competitive spirit in track and orchestra. I dated a little, but had only one serious relationship most of that time. It was postponed when my boyfriend went away to college at the end of my junior year. Little did I know then, that years later, one of his fraternity brothers would look for me in Colorado and eventually ask me to marry him!

After graduation from high school, I attended junior college, and then transferred to a large university. I couldn't believe that there were over 300 people in one of my classes! My world was growing larger. Happily, my family was expanding as well. My sister married and had children, and my brother Bill and his fiancée Lynn were married.

My college studies were interrupted early in the semester of my second year in college when I was involved in a tragic auto accident. I returned to that college a few months later, after recovering from a broken neck. I do remember in the hospital having some of those "one of these days" conversations for the first time...such as I will walk again, feed myself again, drive, and return to school. I did regain it all, and emotional healing as well, thanks to God, my family, friends, physicians and nurses, my physical therapist Deanna at Iowa Lutheran Hospital and my unofficial occupational therapist and angels Dottie and Kathy.

I returned to the university and completed the academic year, then transferred to a local college, graduating a year and half later. After that I moved to Colorado with Jill, a classmate and friend. I began a terrific career in medical administration, and loved my colleagues at the Colorado Foundation for Medical Care. There were many forever friends in beautiful Colorado and special times with my brother and sister in law who also lived there.

Although my career was good, and Colorado was beautiful, it wasn't all roses. I was single and working hard to make ends meet when a roommate's friend visited our apartment and left a cigarette burning. We lost most of what little we had in the ensuing fire. Then I was diagnosed with Leukemia, and had difficult bouts with medicine and testing and expenses...and I was lonely.

An old friend from college days, Jeff, the fraternity brother of my high school boyfriend I mentioned earlier, was working on a temporary project in Denver. He decided to look me up at that time, but had no idea I was right there in Denver. He sent a letter to his mom to forward to me asking for my number. She found my mom and dad's name and address, and sent it in to the family business office to be forwarded. Someone at his family business office misplaced it, but eventually rediscovered it, and forwarded it to mom, who sent it to me in Denver. The timing of all this is just uncanny...or maybe divine intervention. On the last day of Jeff's stay in Denver, I received the letter. I called the job site right away, and he arranged to take me out that evening, I was very happy to see him. We went to the planetarium, a lovely German restaurant in the mountains west of Denver, and then in a blistering snow storm that arose quickly, he kissed me for the first time. He left, but we stayed in touch.

I was a little sad, and surprised to not hear from him for a few weeks, but later discovered that his grandfather had passed away, and he was very involved in taking care of family matters. He sent a dozen red roses to me unexpectedly on Valentine's Day with a simple card simply saying "I love you". I felt overwhelmed with joy. When we talked after that, he asked me to meet some friends in Phoenix where he would be working. His friend Steve, who later became our best man at the wedding, said "Looks like you two belong together". He said he was returning to college in Iowa, and wanted me to be with him, so I agreed to leave Colorado, and transfer to a medical position in West Des Moines, about an hour away. At the end of the year, he was returning to Georgia, and during a short job in Colorado before the move, he invited me out, and asked if I would marry him.

He wasn't a "one of these days" kind of guy, and decided that we should marry six weeks after his proposal. We decided to say our vows at the family church. Roswell United Methodist had a new minister, Reverend Malone Dodson, whom we loved, and we were his first marriage there at the family church. He met with us for premarital counseling, and he said "You two look like you are very much in love, and with strong support from God and family, you're sure to do well". We did have that love and support, and friends and family came from all over the United States to celebrate with us. Since many were not from the south, we had a festive southern themed rehearsal dinner complete with picnic tables on a private lake, his favorite catered barbeque, beer kegs and moonlight.

The wedding and the reception by the Chattahoochee River were beautiful. We began a new life together as man and wife.

When I first moved to Georgia, I had originally wanted to work at the National Center for Disease Control, but we were living in a little cabin at Lake Lanier, and the commute, and very poor hourly pay rate, nixed that idea. I decided to accept a position with a Vascular Surgeon group in Atlanta. Between work, time with his family, church activities, some jazz dancing classes and new friends, I managed to stay busy. Jeff's travel schedule those first years was pretty intense, so staying involved was the right answer.

Three years later, our son Aaron was born. The joy of parenting this miraculous little guy was indescribable. We chose his name from the bible, and apparently it also means "a tower of strength". He has always been that, and has always filled our lives with pride and love. God blessed him in 2002 with a wonderful wife Ashley, and they have two precious children Alex and Brooke. Again, I felt gratitude beyond words. Becoming a parent, was one of the greatest gifts I could have ever imagined. Nothing prepares you for that role. You pretty much learn as you go through trial and error…and more prayers.

Another miracle touched our lives with the birth of our dear daughter Abby. She made the sun shine brighter, and added so much joy to our lives. Abby is driven, creative, and loving; just like her mama some said. She has always had a beautiful mind of her own. She has more talent in many areas than I could have ever imagined. Both of the kids have productive full lives. Actually, I hear that conversation from them a lot…"one of these days" we will get together…still…we do manage to grab some fun and family time whenever we can!

In 1989 I helped David, an engineer, develop his Environmental Engineering business. I spent the next 25 years serving as an independent sales and marketing consultant.

We both worked independently on other ventures over the years as well, but the company stayed intact. It slowed some in later years, with changes in legislation and the economy, but he never gave up. We talked about having a special occasion for the 25th anniversary of his company, but when I asked for a time and date to work on it, he said he hadn't been feeling well at all. I was checking in off and on, but waited to hear from him. When a customer asked if he could be on a site on Monday, I said I would check. His wife called to say that he would not; in fact he had been in the hospital for weeks, and was now going to hospice, where I should come and say my goodbyes.

I was so shocked! I dreaded going there that day, and my heart hurt so deeply for the family. His daughter's wedding was only a few weeks away. I talked with them, hugged a lot, and then leaned over to kiss him on the cheek and say good-bye and 'go with God'. He was already in a coma, but maybe he heard me. He often used to say "Let's pick a time, and we'll have lunch and strategize". So many future plans all disappeared that week for us all.

A few weeks later I took little Brooke to David's daughter's wedding. Brooke was like a ray of sunshine to everyone. "The bride is gorgeous!" she exclaimed, and she danced all evening. God surely shined her little light for all to see that night. I fought back the tears when David's brother danced with his daughter Heather, to the song he had picked; "You are my Sunshine". None of us could have imagined he would not be dancing with her that evening. I suppose he actually was, if angels dance.

One decision I made about nine years ago was to visit my parents more often. I found a way somehow to get there about every four or five months. Mom and dad relocated to a suburb of Austin, Texas in 1989. I recall how much dad loved his work and colleagues and neighbors, and how mom loved her part time work and fellowship with friends in the Midwest. It was hard for them to leave.

Adjusting to retirement, as well as a new life with only one sibling living relatively close, was initially difficult for them. Still, they were grateful for the warmer weather, had many fun times with my older brother and his wife and family, and developed a terrific community of new friends there. A few years later they both faced some major health problems. They were glad that in the previous years they made it to Hawaii, to Whistler, and the northwest regions, because now, they were confined to home for the most part, and their small community. Seeing the love, courage and commitment they have for each other and respect for their vow "in sickness and in health" has been one of the greatest examples I could have ever learned. I have the joy of visiting them two or three times a year. To say I feel gratitude for their presence in my life is an understatement.

Life is not always predictable. We may not always be able to count on getting together later. Nita brought that reality back to me with her words. Some of the people I've long admired are Helen Keller, Mother Teresa, Mom and Dad, my family and a long list of many other strong women and men. Their life examples have encouraged me to live out the rest of my life with passion and purpose "now". I can no longer wait on anything.

Recently I have closed a lot of doors, and some have closed on me, and it is OK. I am easier on myself now, realizing I can't be everything to everyone. I've had an amazing life full of abundance, a variety of interesting careers, charities and international travel. More importantly however, I am grateful for my strong faith and love of family.

Thank you dear Nita for getting me "back on track". I look forward to celebrating your 87th birthday! Would you like to accompany Brooke and me for a whirl on the Atlanta Ferris Wheel? Let's not wait for "one of these days", OK?

Darice Bossen, CHt.

Darice Bossen is a certified clinical hypnotherapist, inspirational speaker and author, and an accomplished lecturer on the subject of human behavior. Originally from Long Island, NY, she moved to the Atlanta area in the late 1970s, where she worked as executive director of an international steel distributor for many years. She attended Georgia State University where she studied Psychology. One day she passed a hypnotherapy clinic and decided to go in and ask about self-improvement. She was so impressed with the results that she quit her corporate career and began training as a hypnotherapist. She has had a thriving practice in Marietta, Georgia for 20 years and has helped thou-

sands of clients accomplish their goals and overcome the obstacles that prevent them from fulfilling their dreams. Darice enjoys cooking and entertaining and she and her husband and their grumpy dachshund Nathan reside in Kennesaw, Georgia.

Contact her through her website at www.reachagoal.com.

Darice's Voice

The Music of My Heart

Darice Bossen, C.Ht.

W e spend most of the bus ride singing, practicing, laughing. The energy is high, and the excitement increases as we reach our destination. The bus pulls to the curb and we fall silent as our attention is drawn to the last minute instructions from our director. He is stern, and his gaze piercing. His eyes graze over us to ensure each and every one of us hears his words. And then he smiles, and in that smile, in that flickering moment, we know he believes we are the best. We are the Sanford H. Calhoun High School Choir from Merrick, NY and he is S. Talbot Thayer. The year is 1970.

Choir robes slung over our arms, we clamor off the bus exploding with anticipation. My classmates and I are about to step onto the stage of the Philharmonic Hall in Lincoln Center to perform "Alexander Nevsky", by composer, Serge Prokofieff. I am 16 years old. A dream is about to come true, an experience I am unfamiliar with.

Dreams do not often come true in my family. My father, filled with such disappointment and discontent with his own life, did everything in his power to squash every dream I ever had. I grew up believing I had no value, no talent, and very little to offer the world. I was stupid, fat and lazy. (In truth, I was none of those things.) He did his best to prove to me why I didn't have what it took to achieve whatever goal I had in mind. Some dreams were literally beaten out of me, others dissipated with the cruelest of words.

On many levels, I believed him, but I also believed that God placed into each of us the knowledge that we are his awesome creation, uniquely made with love. And it is with this knowledge, despite my father's best efforts to the contrary, I continued to dream. And at 15 years old, the dream was to be a singer and a member of the S. H. Calhoun Choir. I love to sing. Music brought peace to my broken soul. God gave me this gift and placed this desire in my heart.

The choir was renowned, and only the cream of the crop were invited to join. The director, S. Talbot Thayer, would only select the best voices, the most dedicated students, and the best attitudes for his choir. To be a member of this elite group was the highest honor to those who love music and love to perform.

The achievement of this dream did not come easy. I auditioned for the choir while in junior high school. That was the first time I met Mr. Thayer, and I was petrified. Of course I was. What made me think I, of little value, had a chance to become a member of this group? And, we all knew his reputation. He demanded excellence and would settle for nothing less. It was well known that his methods of achieving excellence weren't always pleasant. I mustered up all the courage I had and stood before the piano with a group of hopefuls and sang my heart out, trying to pick up on any nuance that he was pleased. He pointed to the girl next to me and said she had perfect pitch. I didn't see anything to pin my hopes on, and I left knowing I did not make it. I was right. A huge part of me knew I wouldn't make it. I was even mocked at home for my efforts. "Don't even try," was the message. "You'll only be disappointed."

So, I started high school singing in the Girls' Chorus, with the other "losers". I was shocked to find out that there were girls in chorus that were content with that, and didn't want to be in "The Choir." There was just something inside that wouldn't allow me to settle for second best. I worked hard in chorus, for there was always the hope that I would shine and Mr. Thayer, who directed this group as well, would see the error he'd made and move me to the choir. Alas, that did not happen and sophomore year ended. In my heart, I reconciled that there would always be next year.

All summer I waited for the acceptance letter from the secretary of the choir welcoming me to my new family. The first day of school arrived and there was still no letter. My heart was heavy with disappointment as I began my junior year with nothing to look forward to. As the class schedules were handed out in homeroom, my stomach did a flip. Maybe my letter was lost in the mail and I would see in the fourth period slot; "Choir". But, NO! There in black and white, were the words I didn't want to see- "Girls Chorus". I didn't make it AGAIN! I knew the chances of ever making it now were slim. Mr. Thayer wouldn't bring you into the choir for senior year, as that would be too late to train you. Another dream had vanished.

One day as the Girls Chorus was practicing songs for our first concert, Mr. Thayer was not happy with what he heard, and for the third time stopped us with "NO, NO, NO! SOPRANOS!", and glared down at them. Their heads were bowed low. The rest of us were so grateful to be altos. He shouted out to us, "Who can tell me what is wrong with them?" Automatically, without conscious thought, I blurt out, "They are sharp."

As soon as the words left my mouth, total regret washed over me. OMG! What did I just do? Mr. Thayer whipped his head around to the direction my voice came from, and with fire in his eyes and asked, "WHO SAID THAT?" Paralyzed with fear, I had no voice. I was too afraid. What if I was wrong? After all, I didn't have "perfect pitch." Now, he might discover I'm not even good enough for girls' chorus. As these thoughts raced through my mind, the heads of my fellow altos turn to me, and I felt all eyes staring at me. I had no choice but to identify myself. As I slowly, cautiously, raised my hand, the fire left his eyes, a smile crossed his lips, and he said, "You are right." He looked at the group and said, "Is she the only one who can hear?" The black cloud that was hanging over my head a moment ago began to evaporate, as if a ray of light emanating from the heavens above began beaming down on me. And if at that moment you listened closely, you could probably hear the choir of angels. I know I did.

The next day, my homeroom teacher told me to report to my guidance counselor. I sat quietly, as he looked at a note on his desk. With a slight smile, he asked me if I wanted to join the choir. "YES!" blurted from my lips, as my brain attempted to catch up. At that moment, my life would never be the same. I stood out amongst the crowd and was chosen. Could the message be that I had something to offer? It was too soon to tell.

I couldn't wait for the day to end. I rushed home from school to share the great news. My mother gave her congratulations and my father told me I'd better not let my grades fall or he would pull me right out. You might say the cheerleading squad at home left something to be desired.

The choir was bustling as we prepared to learn our piece for the Philharmonic Hall performance, and I marveled that I was going to be a part of this. I was fitted for my beautiful blue robe with its silver, satin shawl.

I received my official blue choir folder. On the front, in fancy calligraphy, was printed "S. H. Calhoun Choir," along with my name and member number. I had a number! The folder was filled with the music I had to learn in three weeks. I was certain I would learn it. I was determined. I would not let anyone down. Mr. Thayer told us we were only as good as our weakest link and I would not be that link. I wasn't going to be "deadwood" as he so often shouted at us. Becoming a member gave me a purpose and a direction for my life…it gave me an identity, and now I had a family who accepted me into the fold.

Although I may have been one of the better voices in Girls Chorus, as the newest member of the choir, I was low man on the totem pole, and Mr. Thayer had his favorites. So for me, while the goal had been to be a member of this elite choir, my new goal was to become one of his favorites.

We worked hard during many rehearsals; before school, during and after school, and sometimes after dinner for evening rehearsals. Every minute was spent striving for excellence, and I loved it. The more time we spent rehearsing, the less time I had to be at home. Surrounded by the people who believed we were great, I began to believe I must be great too. And a shift began.

The performance at the Philharmonic was indescribable. Here I was, Darice Blanco, standing on the stage of this magnificent concert hall, with its infamous acoustic white clouds above, singing to a packed house. And I thought to myself, "This is really happening to me!"

As soon as the Philharmonic concert was over, there was little time to reflect on the glory of the moment we had just experienced, because we needed to begin rehearsals for our next concert.

The Christmas Concert is steeped in tradition. Every year, the choir opens the program singing a processional, "O Come, O Come Emanuel" in the hall leading to the auditorium. This year was no exception. As we made our way toward the auditorium, the faint sound of our voices began to drift to the audience. The closer our approach, the louder our voices became. We repeated the verses over and over until we were assembled on the risers. Our director was attired splendidly in his tuxedo, exemplifying the significance of the evening, as he led us in four part harmony. The sound from 100 confident and experienced singers was glorious as the program began.

We sang our way through many Christmas classics. The concert always ends with Handel's Messiah, "The Hallelujah Chorus". The choir lined up in the aisles and the alumni were invited to the risers to join in this celebration. Alumni from graduating classes dating back to 1960 gathered to sing once more under the direction of Mr. Thayer.

Another part of the tradition, and one of my favorite Christmas pieces is "The Twelve Days of Christmas", because it's a fun and beautiful piece, but most importantly because soloists are selected to sing each of the twelve days. To be given a solo part among this group, to be singled out and recognized by Mr. Thayer, was a coveted honor.

Try as I might, I just couldn't seem to move into his circle of "favorites". I worked hard, I was conscientious and dedicated, but I was never chosen for a solo. I had to remind myself that I was a member of the choir, and that in itself was certainly a great achievement.

But this was more than a choir. This was a family and, no matter what else was happening in school, or in your life, when you walked into the choir room you were safe; you were home. Mr. Thayer expected excellence from his chosen choir, and anyone who was a part of it had the ability to be excellent. Through hard work and persistence, we learned we could achieve greatness. He taught us to be strong and to push ourselves even when we thought we had no more to give. Mr. Thayer knew he was instilling these life altering values in us, but what he didn't know was the personal impact he had on my life, and how his words made an indelible mark on my soul.

In the spring of my junior year, I was walking home from school, and Mr. Thayer drove by and asked me if I wanted a ride home. Imagine that happening in this day and age! While my mother's words of caution rang through my head, I decided this was a golden opportunity to speak with him one on one, and I took it. I knew if I was ever going to tell him how much I loved being a member of his choir, it had to be right then. Since we weren't very far from my house, I had to work quickly. I proceeded to pour my heart out. Finally, I asked him why I never impressed him, why he seemed to look right through me. Why was it that after all the days and nights of singing my heart out in his choir, he never noticed me? He listened, silently, as he drove. And then, he shot me a sideways glance and smiled.

"I noticed you. I've seen your dedication and love of music. I've seen your compassion with fellow students, I've seen how willing you are to volunteer, and I've seen your leadership abilities. Darice, you are not a quitter. I noticed it all and I'm sorry you didn't know."

His car slowly pulled to the curb as I pointed out my house. I thanked him for the ride. I really wanted to thank him for so much more, but I was overwhelmed. Later, as the school year was coming to an end, and he was making assignments for the following year's choir, he made me the alto section leader and I was honored. He noticed.

I have reminded myself of those words many times in my life when I doubted myself or my abilities. And I hear his voice in my head, "You are not a quitter". So, for all this, Mr. Thayer, I want to thank you. And to borrow a line from the movie, "Meet Joe Black"," I may not have been your favorite, but you were mine."

Post script:
On June 27, 2015, 190 alumni, traveling from Japan, Israel and all over the United States gathered once again to join voices under the direction of S. Talbot Thayer, and it was sublime. At 85, he is feeling the years bear down on him. But I swear, as we raised our voices after all these years, at least for a moment, he was young again. And so were we.

Elizabeth Buhler Evans

Elizabeth Buhler Evans acquired her RN degree from Perimeter College in 1987 and began her journey at Emory University Hospital caring for Cancer, Bone Marrow Transplant and Kidney Transplant patients. It was there she found herself becoming more involved in the emotional health of each patient. In 1996 she moved on to Gwinnett Medical Center and in 2005 she co-founded Celebrate Recovery in Buford Georgia to offer counseling to those struggling with addictions and co-dependency. In 2007 she was partnered with New Beginnings Counseling Center, becoming Director of Operations in 2008, and in 2014 Elizabeth created Avenues of Life as the president and founder, providing seminars, counseling and coaching throughout the Gainesville area and beyond.

She attended Liberty University Theological Seminary and is a Board Certified Pastoral Counselor, a member of the American Association of Christian Counseling, a member of Hall County Rotary, is certified in Prepare/Enrich for premarital counseling and is accredited by the Georgia Nurses Association in awarding CEU's. She is an author and is in the process of writing her newest marriage and relationship book.

Each year Elizabeth coaches over 1,000 clients and delivers seminars to professionals throughout Georgia. As a life transforming coach, she is in high demand to share her expertise in bringing life into all relationships. She meets clients right where they are by instilling team collaboration for proper boundaries, co-dependency and stress-free relationships at home and in the workplace.

Contact Elizabeth at:
Elizabeth@avenuesoflife.org
Visit her website at:
www.avenuesoflife.org

Elizabeth's Voice

Strive to Thrive!

Elizabeth Buhler Evans

The purpose of my life was to be a wife, mother, friend and sister, but something was missing. I felt there had to more to the big picture. What was I going to be when I grew up? Well, I was already in my forties and I had been a registered nurse since I was 27. Even though I had a profession, I found myself aspiring to new ideas, in order to grow spiritually, emotionally and socially. I felt as though I had so much more to give, and there was so much more to do.

Having felt a great deal of frustration, my mind was overflowing with ideas and questions, yet the life I was living was stale and simple. I felt challenged to seek new avenues of learning, and to give to others in the community, and most importantly, to rise to the challenge of being all God created me to be. In my search for these things I am brought back to this quote…*"God is looking for imperfect men and women who have learned to walk in moment-by-moment dependence on the Holy Spirit; Christians who have come to terms with their inadequacies, fears, and failures. Believers who have become discontent with 'surviving' and have taken the time to investigate everything God has to offer in this life.*"—Charles Stanley

I no longer wanted to just be "content" with surviving, nor did I want to sit around while others did. I wanted something much bigger than me. Better stated "I didn't want it... it wanted me!" But what was *it?* What was this burning in my soul? It had to come out, but I did not know how it would happen. It swelled and kindled as strong as a raging fire. It was so strong and so promising of its hopeful fruition and at the same time I knew it was beyond my power to create it myself. I knew this raging fire would bring me into a closer relationship with Christ, but what would it look like?

This is the story of the voice that made a difference in my life. This was the voice of Bill Franklin. Bill is a pastoral counselor of 30 years, and he helped me in establishing a closer walk with Jesus Christ. His voice led me to Christ at every turn in my journey of learning to give and serve for the glory of God. I didn't have an agenda, except to feed my hunger and thirst for God's word. And then it happened.

There were some things I needed to let go of first.
It was late in the day on a fall day in May. The sun was setting and the evening was closing in. I stood in the grass of my front yard and spoke aloud a decision to drop all that weighed me down...emotionally, spiritually and physically. I brushed my hands together and said, "It is done."

I let it all go, never to be picked up again. I released myself by surrendering my heart, spirit, and soul at the greatest level I had ever imagined. In order to go forward, I had to relinquish the shackles of negative thoughts that were weighing me down.

Through the voice of Bill's spiritual guidance I began to see my rightful heritage and take hold of my freedom as seen in: *"Thus we have been set free to experience our rightful heritage." Galatians 4:4*

What was it for...this day of deliverance? I did not know. For the next six years I would be purged, cleaned and prepared for a greater work with the guidance and help of my mentor. Over time, the power of peace consumed my soul (mind, will and emotions). My soul had been through a war...a spiritual war and it was time to be set free. I couldn't see the war nor could I explain it, but I could feel it. When I shared this spiritual war with others, it was difficult for them to imagine, so I pressed on in faith with the help of Bill's voice of encouragement through scripture: *"I press on toward the goal to win the prize for which God has called me heavenward in Christ Jesus." Philippians 3:14*

In the process of being set free in peace, I was able to see that no man or woman could stand in God's way. The day I made a decision to give up myself and lean into the power of the glory and grace of the one true God, peace washed over me. This peace was not easily received by those in my life and even loved ones who were used to living in a degree of unrest and lack of peace.

This type of resolve I was experiencing was a crucial and pivotal point in my life; a time where a new life could and would begin. I could not do it alone. I continued to lean on the Holy Spirit and communicate with my mentor, Bill. He was a man who spoke the truth through scriptures at every turn of a conversation. I allowed him to speak into my life concerning the groaning and desires of my heart in the search for a deeper relationship with Christ.

He taught me that my heart was a reflection of my mind and vice versa. What I thought was what was in my heart and what

I felt was due to what was on my mind. I learned the power of my mind and heart feeding each other. Bill was able to help me see what I was feeding my mind and heart. The fact is...I wasn't feeding it the promises of my maker and the true love God had for me.

Bill conveyed the significance of my life through Christ's eyes to me. He did this by showing me how to become rooted in the word of God..."by seeing my roots in Christ."

So, we began with *How beautiful I am to Christ and how I was born from an imperishable seed, as in 1st Peter 1:22-23.*

As I read the scriptures I was deeply strengthened in Christ. It was amazing!

Instead of living my life in fear, I chose to live my life in peace and love. Most of us live in fear and don't even realize it. The struggle most of us deal with is the battle between...

"Fear and Love"

There were people in close relationships with me that did not support my desire to be all I could be in Christ. My loved ones were comfortable seeing me the way they wanted to see me, and imposed this viewpoint on me daily. This caused fear in my life. In trying to please them, I was not being true to who I was personally and in my relationship with Christ. This was not comfortable for me. I soon learned of God's great power over all he ordains, including his plan for my life and for yours. Soon after learning this I chose to no longer be punished for wanting to believe in God's promises for me. I chose love over fear in my journey of being all I could be in Christ. I decided to be perfect in love, casting out my fears based on other's insecurities and fears.

"There is no fear in love. But perfect love drives out fear, because fear has to do with punishment. The one who fears is not made perfect in love." 1 John 4:18

Growing up and struggling without a constant parental figure, I had no idea of the peace I could experience from surrendering to Christ my father. Not knowing how important I was to Christ kept me from receiving the gift of peace and the assurance of being His daughter. I hope the following scripture will fill you with confidence in Christ and bring you the peace it gave me along my journey.

"You can tell for sure that you are now fully adopted as his own children because God sent the Spirit of his Son into our lives crying out, "Papa! Father!" Galatians 4:5-6

This was very good news to me, and quite the prize! You see, growing up my loved ones made a lot of negative statements about who I was, and unaware of how that affected my thinking, over time it devalued my feelings as a person in different areas of my life. This fed the negative thoughts in my head, causing fear and conflict as I tried to please people I loved. But a new knowledge came to me during these six years.

Throughout the years, Bill has continued to mentor me and teach me the Bible. It was as if I were being prepared for some-thing bigger in my life, even though I did not know what it was. I soaked up every bit of wisdom, just the same. I could call him and tell him a problem or concern, and he would take me straight to scripture. It was as if he knew no mortal words could answer my concerns better than the word of God. He was correct.

As the years went by, he continued to share scripture, and challenged me with homework. I remember him asking me to write a 1500 word paper on the seven "I Am's of Jesus," and I did. I still have it today. There were many exercises like this that helped me to develop into who I am today. You see, by knowing who Jesus is more intimately, I grew to know more about who I was, in Him. It was invaluable.

On many occasions he had me read Galatians, which today is probably the source of most of the wisdom I share with my clients. It is ingrained in my heart, and allows me to help so many, as it naturally flows from my tongue in conversation with those who are searching. This particular scripture is in Galatians…

"Am I now trying to win the approval of human beings, or of God? Or am I trying to please people? If I were still trying to please people, I would not be a servant of Christ" Galatians 1:10

This means I will only live for God and I don't have to fear man. This is the one scripture that, due to Bill's help in my life; I am able to share with my clients. It's as if a light bulb goes off when they hear it; they don't have to live for others. So many people who come to my office struggle with pleasing others and feel trapped. It is known as codependency, or as Bill more accurately stated, "Idolatry." This is quite a phenomenon. Those who struggle to live with someone who wants to mold them into something they are not often find themselves troubled and unhappy.

I learned that when two people communicate with each other, whether at work or at home, it works out best when they are left to be who they were created to be. This is the basis of a healthy relationship. Let me share a good quote for most relationships-

"What women rightly long for is spiritual and moral initiative from a man, not spiritual and moral domination."—John Piper

Even on the job, no matter the gender, there should be no domination, only spiritual and moral initiative.

My parents passed away in my early adulthood. They were never really available to me as leaders or advisors, so I gathered and savored many blessings and words of wisdom from my mentors. For this season of my life, Bill has been the mentor who had answers for many of the questions I had about life. He showed me…I am Christ's daughter!

"So in Christ Jesus you are all children of God through faith" Galatians 3:26

More importantly, he assured me of who I was in Christ. Yes, I am Christ's ambassador and so are you.

"We are therefore Christ's ambassadors, as though God were making his appeal through us. We implore you on Christ's behalf: Be reconciled to God." 2nd Corinthians 5:20

In troubling times, Bill reminded me of God's provision for safety over me…

"If I climb to the sky, you're there!"
"If I go underground, you're there!"
Psalm 139: 2
"Oh, he even sees me in the dark!
At night I'm immersed in the light!"
Psalm 139:11

"Take great comfort in knowing God always has you in mind and is overseeing your safety," Bill would tell me. I know everyone needs to hear this. This took place between 2002 and 2004.

In spending close to four hours a day in the presence of God, I was filled with comfort and peace. Jesus was my husband for the very first time, and it was glorious and stunning all at the same time. He revealed the significance of the word of God to me through this scripture…

"Therefore, there is now no condemnation for those who are in Christ Jesus, because through Christ Jesus the law of the Spirit who gives life has set you free from the law of sin and death. For what the law was powerless to do because it was weakened by the flesh, God did by sending his own Son in the likeness of sinful flesh to be a sin offering. And so he condemned sin in the flesh, in order that the righteous requirement of the law might be fully met in us, who do not live according to the flesh but according to the Spirit. Romans 8:1-4

Bill taught me to live in the spirit and by the spirit. I had never grasped this until...well not even then! I still did not get it. It wasn't't until the next year that I really got it, and was not expecting to. I went on a retreat and came back very aware of speaking boldly in the spirit. Having increased confidence in God and myself filled me with the greatest sense of peace that I had ever known.

By now it was 2005 and I had been gleaning wisdom from Bill for three years. One morning, at my usual 3a.m. Prayer time... the *call* to speak came! Getting up at this hour had been the time I would ordinarily awaken in the middle of the night and pray myself back to sleep in my "prayer closet" with my bible. This became an every night occurrence for many years, and was something I looked forward to. I never expected to receive this kind of call, but I was on board. As I spoke of this burning desire to a loved one about serving others and the call to speak about Christ, I was told "No way in hell you are going into full time ministry!" I was devastated and went back to the prayer closet and continued leading bible classes on the word of God and boundaries.

That same year in 2005 I was asked to help start 'Celebrate Recovery' in Buford Georgia, and I gladly did so. I began taking classes in Biblical Studies, and in 2007 I started counseling as a Pastoral Counselor with New Beginning Counseling Center. Counseling was so natural; I felt as though this was what I was born to do. I loved it and remembered scripture Bill taught me...

"Not looking to your own interests but each of you to the interests of the others." Philippians 2:4

Throughout the last couple of years my son Jeremiah and I would talk about monkeys, so I authored a book, "The Adventures of Tizzy." Dr. Stanley at Spellman College said "It's a great children's book, but you better be ready, because the kids will want more." This endeavor was met with opposition by a loved one in my life; however I persevered in not fearing *man*. This loved one in opposition was fearful of my being all I could be in Christ and told me I should have never visited an editor without asking permission first. I continued to love and live in peace as I prayed for this loved one to not live in fear and to have faith in Christ.

In 2012 I went on a mission trip to Guatemala where our team ministered to those living in an area near the city dump, and we saw a great deliverance in the lives of those who were open for growing in Christ.

I met and married George Evans in 2013, wrote four more Tizzy books which George illustrated, and in 2014 I started Avenues of Life Counseling and Coaching in Gainesville Georgia. Now in 2015, when I speak to groups and work in counseling, I think back to all Bill taught me about who I am in Christ. I now have the honor and privilege to share it with the rest of the world. I know the Holy Spirit will speak for me and He will speak through me.

Matthew 10:19 *"But when they arrest you, do not worry about what to say or how to say it. At that time you will be given what to say."* Matthew 10:19-20

Bill was stricken with cancer, but thankfully he won that battle, and he is available once again to those who are seeking wisdom in the word of Christ. Thank you and God bless you, Bill Franklin. for your faith and prayers. Thank you for your tireless teaching of God's word, and your dedication to me and others yet to come.

Tina Greer

Business Growth Strategist / Speaker / Author

Tina Greer is a successful corporate business woman, entrepreneur, speaker and author. She received her Bachelor of Science in Business Administration from Southern Illinois University-Edwardsville, IL. In addition, she completed her Master of Public Administration from Murray State University, Murray, KY.

She has over 20 years of experience in business management, finance, and business development. She is the CEO of Greer Business Solutions, LLC, founder of Sisters United, and owner of Affirmations for the Soul™ inspirational products and mer-

chandise. She has a passion for helping others succeed in business and in life!

For more information:

Visit www.tinagreer.com

Email: info@tinagreer.com

Office: 678-561-6704

Facebook.com/
affirmations4thesoul

Facebook.com/
greerbusinesssolutions

Tina's Voice

The Voices That Transcend Through Generations

Tina Greer

As a young child growing up, I remember how my grandmother was the nucleus of the family. She was a strong African American woman whose birthplace was in Grenada, Mississippi. She was the daughter of Ruby Thelma and Edgar Anderson. Back then families were large; her family consisted of eleven biological brothers and sisters, of which two sisters were paternal twins. My grandmother was called "Ma Dear", which is short for Mother Dear. Her birth name is Louise Anderson.

My grandmother was a God-fearing woman. She raised nine children as a single parent in the 50's and 60's. When her sister passed away unexpectedly, she adopted her sister's seven children and raised them as her own. Can you imagine how much strength, love, and compassion she had for her family? That is why I love her so much. She did not think about the challenges she would face raising sixteen kids; this is just what she was called to do. She was the matriarch of the family. With all of the challenges she faced raising sixteen kids in the civil rights era, she still maintained a well kept home. She was the only financial provider in the family. Can you imagine raising nine children in today's economy, let alone taking in seven more on top of that, and being the sole provider?

My grandmother was a survivor. She loved helping people. She received her Nurse's Aide Certificate in the sixties from Lincoln Technical Center, Venice, IL and worked at Madison County Nursing Home as a nurse's aide for many years until her retirement. She had a heart for helping others.

As a child growing up in Illinois, I used to enjoy Sunday dinners at my grandmother's house. That is when we enjoyed a home-cooked meal made from scratch. Everyone gathered after church services to eat her delicious cooking. We called my grandmother's cooking "Soul" food. She would make dishes such as macaroni and cheese, fried chicken, collard greens, dumplings, homemade cornbread, potato salad, peach cobbler, and so much more. Just thinking about all her delicious food makes my mouth water!

My grandmother made special dishes from the leftovers. She was so talented and gifted in the kitchen, and she did not waste a thing. Remember, she had to be efficient in providing good meals because she had so many mouths to feed in her large family.

All of the food was prepared before Sunday morning services, so when she returned home from church, the food was ready. The entire family sat down at the dinner table and broke bread together. There was a multitude of conversations filling the room with laughter, fun, and excitement! The TV was not on. There were no smart phones, laptops, or iPads to distract us. We were truly present in the conversations.

As I look back over my childhood, I remember my grand-mother as a gentle person, who loved the Lord and could pray with such power in her voice. She always had a smile on her face. I remember when she let me braid her hair. She had such beautiful thick black wavy hair growing down past her shoulders, and it was chemical free; no perms or straighteners. I have never seen such beautiful hair. My grandmother was one of a kind. A true Proverbs 31 woman, as written in the Bible!

My mother Anna told me that, as a child, in order to be able to maintain order in the house, there had to be rules and sys-tems in place. Each child was responsible for completing their assigned chores and responsibilities. Each sibling looked out for one another. My grandmother made sure everyone had what they needed, including food, clothes, and a place to call home. My mother always told me how much fun they had growing up. They never wanted for anything. My grandmother was also a seamstress, so she knew how to make the children's clothes and stitch them up when necessary. They were always properly dressed for school. By all accounts, the children grew up in a loving environment.

My grandmother was very special to me. She embodied strength, courage, love, tenacity, and confidence. She was a respected woman in her local community, church, and in the medical community. She disciplined her children so they would know the difference between right and wrong and they listened and respected her authority.

We had a family reunion every year in a different state based upon where the host family resided. To offset the cost of attending such an event, my grandmother made sure she took as many of our family members as she could with her, so they could attend the reunion at no cost. She provided the financial resources so relatives could be there who otherwise could not have gone.

I remember when grandmother took me on my first airplane ride to Virginia. I still remember looking out of the window of the plane, watching the clouds as we travelled, in awe of the beauty.

My grandmother was a safe haven for all. She loved her family and community. Friends would call her Ms. Louise, but to me she was just "Ma Dear". Her character and grace were an inspiration to many people.

When I was a sophomore in college, my grandmother co-signed a loan with no hesitation so I could buy my first car. That was a big deal to me. She believed in me as a responsible young adult.

When I completed my undergraduate degree and moved to Washington, DC with my fiancé, Roy Greer, it was important for me to receive her blessing. I knew she wanted me to be married before moving in with him, but she accepted that I was growing up as a young adult and finding my own way at the age of 24. I have been married to Roy for over 21 years now. I respected my grandmother so much, and she believed in me to do the right things in life. I know she would be proud of the woman that I have become. She exuded strength, perseverance, faith in God, and love. These qualities, I know, have been passed down to me to shape my future. There are not a lot of "Ma Dear's" left in today's society. I am blessed to have had such a wonderful grandmother, and can truly say I miss her and love her with all my heart.

Grandma, thank you for shining the light and letting me know that I have greatness within me, and that I can do all things through Christ who strengthens me!

There is a legacy of voices that impacted my life and shaped me to be the woman I am today. This legacy included not only my grandmother, but my mother as well.

Her name is Anna Claggett. Here is a little known fact; my grandmother, mother, and I share the same zodiac sign. We are all Virgos. Interestingly enough, my oldest daughter is a Virgo too!

As a single parent, my mother also exuded the qualities of strength, tenacity, and courage as she raised me and my three brothers. Some people tell me "you had it made" or "you were spoiled." That is truly not the case. My mother, in my opinion, was harder on me as a girl growing up than she was on my three brothers. She taught me to be self reliant and independent. She taught me how to be a young lady and treat others with kindness and respect. As for etiquette, we were taught that respect was earned, not given. We always showed respect for our elders. We would address them with "yes ma'am" or "no ma'am", and "yes sir" or "no sir". We also were taught to use proper English when addressing others.

In today's society, we do not see or hear this as much as we would like to, especially in the social media world. However, the notion of "training up a child" is still in effect today. It all starts at home in a loving, caring environment. Raising men is no easy task in today's society, or even back in the 70's and 80's. My mother did the best she could, especially since there was no consistent adult male presence in the home.

One of my favorite holidays was Easter. My mother purchased two Easter dresses for me, which was our tradition. I wore one at our regular church service and the other for our Easter program that evening at church, where I recited my Easter poem. We had some fun times growing up. We were involved with the

Youth Department of my home church, New Salem Baptist, and participated in all of the fun activities.

We were not born with a silver spoon; however, we had what we needed. My mother worked hard to provide for us. She has worked in the health care industry for over 40 years, and she loves the world of science and the study of scientific laboratory techniques including micro-biology, hematology, chemistry, serology, urinalysis, and phlebotomy. The health care field was never an interest of mine. I am partial to the business world, but my oldest daughter is currently in college majoring in biology with plans to attend veterinary college and become a veterinarian.

My mother is very active in her church and she was also very active in the Booster Club as well as the Parks and Recreation Board in our local community. She truly believes in our youth and strives to keep them active in the community through various programs she helped to implement. From holding cheerleading camps, to organizing activities for the local park, my mother loves working with young people.

She is such supportive person. I remember my freshman year in college, I had a part in the college play and my mother drove for four hours to come watch my "performance." I am going to tell you, my part consisted of just two words, repeated three times. In my best theatrical voice, I delivered my line "I want, I want, I want!"—that's it, all done. We joke about it all the time and just laugh, and my mother will tease "I drove all the way there just to here you say that!", with a bellowing laugh and smile. Now that is love. How many people would travel so far to hear you say so little?

My mother believes in the importance of education. She graduated with her Bachelor of Arts degree in 1997. That was a proud moment! My mother loves to learn new things and wanted to reach the milestone of receiving her degree. Seeing my mother graduate from the university taught me that you are never too old to pursue your dreams and goals. My mother put her desires on the back burner for many years to make sure we had everything we needed so we could succeed in college. Only then did she begin her own college studies. I was so proud when my mother received her degree! That just reinforced in me the belief that we can achieve anything when we put our minds to it. With hard work, dedication, and focus, it is possible!

I believe that you should give flowers to the ones that impact your life while they are still living. Even though my grandmother is no longer with us, my mother is still here, and I want her to know that I appreciate the support and love she has given to me and my family. She is a caring person just like grandmother, and her siblings look up to her with respect and love. She is always willing to give her last dime to make sure we are happy and have what we need. She is known for giving back to the community, and for service to others.

My mother equipped me with the tools I need to raise two beautiful young women, women who have the drive and passion to succeed in life. Thank you for instilling that in me!

No matter where I have lived in my adult life (and I have lived in many states), my mother has always found the time to come visit me and my family. My mother is adventurous and is willing to try new things. We have so many more trips we plan to take together. Mother, I want to continue to explore the world with you. There is so much for us to do and see as a family. If you are willing, game on! We are continuing to write our story and the best is yet to come!

The voices that changed everything transcend the generations. It started with my grandmother, Louise Anderson; then my mother, Anna Claggett. Those teachings and words of wisdom are now engrained in my soul. I will never forget the impact you both made on my life and are still making today. You are both role models to me and your examples let me know that there is always a way to succeed; to continue to fight to get what you deserve, to never give up, and to strive for the best! You have shown me what it is to become successful. Success can mean raising good children, having a strong work ethic, being able to complete school (no matter the age, nor how long it takes to obtain the degree), and leaving a financial legacy for the family.

Mother, you are our best supporter and you always have our back. You love us unconditionally and accept our shortcomings and correct us when we are wrong. You taught us the right way to handle any situation. Even though my father was not there, you made sure I had a male presence in my life through the support of my uncles. I appreciate that. I love you and I just want to say that your voice will always resonate with me. Thank you for being present in my life and continuing to give me love, guidance, and support.

Aimee Oczkowski

Aimee Oczkowski is a Juice Plus+ Virtual Franchise Owner and founder of Aim4GoodHealth, LLC. Family roots in North Georgia brought her as a teen to the Atlanta area in 1989. Aimee attended Kennesaw State College (now University) and worked in a doctor's office where she quickly found her niche in Information Technology (IT) and worked her way up to the IT department as a trainer and help desk technician. From there she got a job with Internet Security Systems (ISS) in Technical Support in 1998. Aimee began to focus on her career, successfully moving up the corporate ladder in the IT industry. She chose to further herself by finishing school, where she graduated from AIU summa cum

laude with a Bachelor's Degree in Information Technology in 2004, and received an MBA in Management in 2005. In 2006, when the ladder became narrower at the top with fewer positions and more competition the only way to get to the next level was for her to move to a new company as Director of Technical Support and Education. Shortly after doing so,

God decided He had bigger plans and she became a Stay-at-Home Mom in 2007. Having 3 wonderful children over the course of 5 years, Aimee lovingly focused all of her attention on her family but neglected her own health and wellness. She describes her situation as "having lost herself" until she met "The Voice That Changed Everything" in July, 2014. With a new found passion to Aim4GoodHealth, Aimee is now mission driven to help families get healthy and help moms like herself find themselves again.

Connect with Aimee! She would love to hear from you!
email aimee@aim4goodhealth.com
web www.Aim4GoodHealth.com
Facebook Fan Pages: Aim4GoodHealth, LLC
& Aim4HealthyKids
@Aim4GoodHealth on Instagram
and @Aim4HealthyKids on Twitter

Aimee's Voice

Legoland Change-Oland

Aimee Oczkowski

In 1996, my mom's friend handed us some sort of weird capsules and said, "Here! Eat these fruits and vegetables in a capsule. It'll make you feel good." OK, sure! Why not? Little did we know just how good these "magic beans" would make my mom and me feel, or that they were capable of creating amazing balance in our bodies!

I was in my early 20's when we started eating these "magic beans". I struggled with my weight all my life, so I was willing to try anything in order to lose those 25lbs that just wouldn't go away. I ate them for almost a year, and back then I didn't know why I suddenly had so much energy, or why I craved more fruits and vegetables and less "junk" food, or even why I loved drinking water over anything else. I found that I was able to work full-time, go to school, workout on a regular basis and go out dancing with friends until the wee hours of the morning. I did this several nights during the week. I was in my 20's, and that's what it's supposed to be like in your 20's, right? When I asked my mom what she remembered I was like before the "magic beans", she told me I was always tired, slept the weekends away, just went to work and school, and only went out with friends on Saturday nights. Twenty-somethings aren't supposed to need "magic beans" to have that much energy or to stay healthy.

Who am I kidding? Yes they do!! Because we ALL need more fruits and vegetables to improve our health. We honestly didn't realize during that year of eating our "magic beans" that we were actually eating concentrated fruits and vegetables. I know now that those "magic beans" were responsible for my desire to exercise (as a result of all my extra energy), as well as my desire to eat healthier and drink water, which resulted in the natural weight loss I experienced. But for whatever reason we stopped eating our "magic beans", and I reverted to old bad habits over the course of the next 20 years. Things started to go downhill for me and I gained those 25 pounds back fairly quickly, and then some...and then some more...and some more, until I was well over 200 pounds. Every time I tried to lose some of the weight, I gained it back, plus 10 pounds more.

And every time I lost a little weight, I stalled, and I got more and more discouraged; I had less and less willpower, and I finally gave up and settled for where I was. I know that I am not the only one in this boat, so there's no need to pretend that "nobody understands what it's like." For the sake of helping someone else, I'm going to be very transparent with you. My license says 170lb—yeah, I haven't see that number on the scales since 1996!

In 2006, I was determined to lose this weight once and for all. I started (another) "quick weight loss program" and got down to 210 pounds! Woo-hoo! That was 3 pounds smaller than I was when my husband and I got married in 2001! With my newly shrinking body, my new college degree and MBA, my more confident attitude, and my new clothes, I set out to get a new job and landed it! A new job also meant that my husband and I needed to quickly take that Hawaiian vacation that we vowed we would go on, because I wasn't going to be taking another vacation any time soon.

The day before starting my new executive level job, I found out I was pregnant. God had bigger plans for me, and those plans didn't include the career path that I had been focusing on. I was happy about the pregnancy because we had been trying for over a year, but it happened just as I landed a new job. I kept it a secret for as long as I could, but there were unavoidable doctor's appointments and well, there was the obvious—my body was changing! Just before my 90-day probation period ended, I had to let someone know I had an urgent appointment, and that person betrayed my trust. Things started to become weird around the office and I thought it best to be honest with my boss. My position was conveniently "eliminated" just 2 weeks after the CEO found out I was pregnant.

I'd never been "fired" before and I used to wonder why I wasn't disappointed about it, but I don't live in that space. My old company let me come back part-time as a contractor. I have always had faith that things happen for a reason. I believe this happened because I was working so hard and was so stressed out that my baby was not growing properly. I ended up with pre-eclampsia and high blood pressure and my daughter was born 5 weeks early. She was perfectly healthy, just a little ahead of schedule. It was all part of God's bigger plan.

I instantly became a stay-at-home mom and pretty much got it in my head that I wasn't going back to that type of corporate environment—ever. (But don't tell my husband…<wink!>) In

2010, I had a son. While that was the easiest pregnancy of all three of my children, I was not as healthy as I could have or should have been. I was 237 pounds when he was born, and again I ended up with high-blood pressure that landed me back in the ER just two days after bringing him home.

When my son was three months old, our family had two huge scares. My brother (44 years old at the time) had to have a quintuple bypass as a result of his scleroderma, but regardless, I looked at that as a wakeup call to myself. And when my other brother (46 years old at the time) was diagnosed with serious heart damage requiring a defibrillator in his chest, I became terrified that something was going to happen to me, too. It was time for me to get serious about my health! I returned to a well-known weight loss program for the umpteenth time, this time getting down to 222 pounds. And darn if it didn't happen again! Yep! I started gaining the weight back!

In 2012, I got pregnant with number three and weighed somewhere just over 235 pounds. I was put on home bed rest for six months because my blood pressure had crept up, and we were trying to keep me out of the hospital as long as possible and away from pre-eclampsia. If the meaning of "bed rest" is unclear to you it means laying down on your left side all day and all night. I was allowed to get up to use the bathroom (because you're also required to drink water, water, water!) and shower every other day or so. I could not get up to cook, clean, do laundry, or take care of the other two young children. Thank goodness I had an awesome mom and husband! I did finally end up on "hospital bed rest" for the last two weeks. We were holding out as long as we could to get to 37 weeks. She was born in December, and I was the heaviest I've ever been—pushing 260 pounds. And I again ended up back in the ER with extremely high blood pressure after we came home.

For 20 months I battled to survive a vicious cycle of depression, anxiety, nightly panic attacks, fatigue, "junk-food-addiction", "couch-potato" syndrome and what I now know was an extremely toxic body, because I was going nowhere with my up and down weight and health. With my family history constantly at the front of my mind, I laid awake every night having panic attacks because I just knew that I was going to die in my sleep.

Sleepless nights and too much adrenaline in my system from anxiety created exhaustion. I didn't have energy to do anything. My husband got upset with me because laundry piled up and the dishwasher wasn't emptied, if it had even been started at all. He wanted to help and he would ask me what he could do for me, but I shut him and everyone else out. Fighting and yelling became "normal," but I knew I didn't want to live like that. I thought I was going crazy; I just needed to deal with this myself. I even tried to eat healthier, but it was just too exhausting and the junk food tasted so much better.

I withdrew from family and friends. They knew something wasn't right, but didn't know what it was. They didn't know what to say to me. I had to force myself to get up, get out and do things with the kids every day. This was the only thing that kept me from going crazy, but it was also the only thing I was capable of doing.

It was painful on so many levels. I constantly asked myself, "What is wrong with me?! I love being a mom. I am grateful and blessed that I have such an amazing husband who supports me and allows me to be a stay-at-home mom. But who have I become?" I didn't feel like me, but I didn't know who "me" was anymore.

I was lost. I was stuck. I was fat. I was sick. I thought was I was going to die. Again, I know I am not the only person on the boat who's been stuck in these rapids. Where do you go for help?

I went to see my doctor. He suggested seeing a therapist, and possibly going on medication to help with the depression and anxiety. I saw a therapist, but she wasn't right for me. Perhaps the timing was off. I tried Zoloft for a week. That made me sick to my stomach and gave me bad dreams. I'm never doing that again! I prayed to God, and tried to make it through each day with gratitude, but that was really tough.

During this 20 month period I also had to deal with the guilt that my oldest daughter was found to have higher cholesterol at age six than I did at 40, even with me being obese! I carry this guilt because I am responsible for making sure she and my other two children have a healthy diet. Fast food was more convenient and pretty cheap, and remember, I didn't feel like doing anything. My husband's health declined, too. He was diagnosed with type 2 diabetes in March, 2014. He has never been overweight! I am the obese one! What am I doing to my family? I prayed to God, "Please! Please help me find a solution!" I realized that if I didn't get my family's health under control, we would all suffer with heart disease, diabetes, and obesity for the rest of our lives. My daughter was in serious danger of having to be put on cholesterol lowering medication in the not too distant future if something didn't change. How could this happen?

One day in April, after another one of those days where I had to force myself out of the house so the kids could have a play-date, someone mentioned putting their kids on a product called Juice Plus+. She said it helped her kids to eat more fruits and vegetables. She suggested maybe it would help my daughter, who only liked to eat beige food—no fruit or veggies—well, maybe an occasional slice of apple or two, but no skin!

Juice Plus+ sounded really familiar. Was that the product my mom's friend gave me back in my early 20's? Is that stuff still around? She had her representative call me, and I said I'd look into it, but she never followed up with me and it got pushed to the back of my mind.

And then something A-MAZ-ING happened to me—God stepped in and answered my prayers.

I remember the day like it was yesterday. It was July 21, 2014 at around 2:30 in the afternoon. I had taken my kids to LEGOLAND because school was starting in a couple of weeks and I promised them we would go. It was another one of those forced days out of the house. I was sitting on a stool watching my youngest child playing with the LEGOS, while the oldest two were on the playground, climbing around and having fun. There was an empty stool next to me and a lady asked if she could sit down. I said, "Sure."

What happened next was such divine intervention that nobody could have made this up. She started a casual conversation with me, asking how long I had been at LEGOLAND that day. Being polite, I returned the question. Then she asked, "Where did you drive from?" I told her the name of my suburb north of Atlanta and she said, "OH! Me too!" It turned out that we live only ten minutes from each other.

As we continued our conversation, we exchanged names. She recognized "Oczkowski" and remembered seeing that name somewhere. I told her, "You probably recognize it from when my husband ran for office in 2010." We had two billboards up on the main road with his picture, and with a name like "OCZKOWSKI" in North Georgia, it's kind of easy to recognize. We were finding more and more common ground, and found that we knew some of the same people, one of whom had just recently passed away from a massive heartache. Our mutual friend was also involved in the political circle in our community and I had known him well. I told her how sad I was to hear of his passing because it was so sudden. Then my new friend, Susan Cannizzaro said, "Yeah, I know. I tried getting him on Juice Plus+ for years, and he finally did, but it was too late."

At that moment, my mind opened up and God was speaking to me so I spoke back in my head. I said, "OK God, are you trying to tell me something? If so, will she ask me if I've ever heard of Juice Plus+ before?"

The very next question out of Susan's mouth was, "Have you ever heard of Juice Plus+?"

This is 100%, without a doubt, a sign from God.

"As a matter of fact I have."

This was the answer to my prayers. Within the week, Susan provided me with all the information I needed to know about these concentrated fruits and vegetables and I decided that I needed to figure out how to make this work. I was determined to get my family healthy once and for all.

She even introduced me to the business side of Juice Plus+, showing me how easy it was to share this with other people, so I could earn just enough to pay for my own family's products. If I decided to, I could even make this a successful business. Susan Cannizzaro is the VOICE THAT CHANGED EVERYTHING for me. She is encouraging. She is compassionate and kind. She is a good friend and mentor. God placed her in my life as the beacon of hope, a beacon that has opened my heart, my mind and my soul to better way of health and wealth for me and my family.

I have not experienced an anxiety attack since July 28, 2014. And since the day that Susan sat down next to me at LEGOLAND and re-introduced me to my "magic beans", I no longer battle that vicious, unhealthy cycle. I naturally stopped craving sugar. I naturally started drinking more water. I naturally had the energy to get up and go, to do things with and for my family.

I naturally crave more fruits and veggies. My body is finally working the way it was designed to and I am once again getting healthier and losing weight naturally every day. I no longer feel deprived, or that I must cut out every bad habit at once. I make one simple change at a time so they become healthy, sustainable habits. For me, making one change at a time keeps me focused on my target to Aim4GoodHealth, and through this process I stopped just "surviving" and I started LIVING!

I am also happy to tell you that my daughter's cholesterol returned to a normal range after just a few months of eating Juice Plus+. She now eats more fruits and veggies and is willing to at least try new things. She is finding that healthy food choices make her feel better. My other two children are still young enough that they don't remember eating unhealthy food, and this new healthy lifestyle is just part of who they are now.

I shudder to think where my family would be if Susan hadn't been bold enough to share her passion for Juice Plus+ with me, AND she inspired me to do the same for other women who feel as helpless as I did! I love giving hope to Moms like me!

I finally found my purpose—this is God's plan for me. And for all this, I am grateful.

Leslie McElhannon

Leslie was born in Tennessee and has always been a Volunteer at heart. She was Salutatorian of her high school class (Lebanon Blue Devils), attended Cumberland University on a full ride scholarship, and then went on from there to the top ten rated MAcc program at University of Tennessee, Knoxville where she graduated with honors.

She has worked for some exciting companies such as Whittle Communications and Blimpie as well as several regional accounting firms, where she was a CPA and aspired to partner status. Her career path has taken her from the West Coast to the Midwest to the Midsouth of Atlanta where she has settled with her

husband and high school sweetheart, David.

Currently, she is working her Mary Kay business, which is both satisfying and profitable. With a goal to be a National Sales Director, sometimes her days are pretty hectic. She also gives part of her time to charity, working with Voice Today and Senior Services of North Fulton. Her two

Yorkshire Terriers, Goliath and Razzle Dazzle help her daily to keep perspective about what is important in life, as does her time alone with God. She has adopted the gold standard of God first, family second, and career third, which is about as balanced an approach to life as one can get.

Contact Leslie:
Leslie McElhannon
Mary Kay Independent Beauty Consultant
678-908-8699
Lmcelhannon@marykay.com
www.marykay.com/Lmcelhannon
www.facebook.com/LeslieMcelhannon.consultant

Leslie's Voice

A Gentle Clear Voice

Leslie McElhannon

Have you ever been so consumed with what you wanted that you couldn't see anything else? This happens to a lot of people, maybe even you! For me, it was work, work, and more work. At least, that is how it seemed to me. I was good at my job, but it was consuming my life. I demanded excellence of myself, and I was well on my way to achieving success. But then, unexpectedly, a voice spoke to me and gave me clarity. Did it scream at me? Was it thunderous in volume? It doesn't always happen that way. Sometimes, you have to listen with your heart. I listened, and because I did, everything in my life got better. I hope you will listen as well.

One day when I was in college, my father wanted to talk with me. He told me that I didn't have to work both a full and part-time job while going to school full-time and participating in school activities. He could provide for all my needs. I told him that I appreciated his kindness, but I had wants. That was why I had to work two jobs (or so I thought). My parents had provided what I *needed*, but not all the things I *wanted*. We were a blue-collar middle class family. I should have listened, but I was already going down that road.

I was also an obsessive planner (I had plans A, B, C, and so on) my life plan "A" was to be a woman partner in a CPA (Certified Public Accounting) firm. To accomplish plan "A", once I completed my Masters and passed the CPA exam, I needed to find a job working as an apprentice under a CPA for a minimum of two years in order to qualify for a license.

Initially, I worked in the corporate environment in Knoxville, Tennessee, biding my time. I knew that I would be moving to the Los Angeles, California area, where my husband had taken a job. It was during this move that I would focus on getting a job in a CPA firm. My husband had already moved to LA six months earlier, while I stayed in Tennessee to help my boss, who was going out on maternity leave. I was going to fill in for her, and pick up some managerial experience to build my resume. Was that the best plan for a newlywed? Honestly, I was not thinking of that. I had my plan and was working it no matter what.

The move to California was quite a transition for someone who grew up in Tennessee. Outside of the obvious culture shock, I moved from a state with no state income tax to one that had one of the most complicated state tax systems in the United States. After being in California for just few months, I received an interview and an offer from a CPA firm to be tax accountant. This firm specialized in HOA (Homeowner's Associations) audits and did taxes on the side. It's funny that I got a job doing taxes, and not audits, since I really did not want to do taxes. When you need and want a job to complete your licensing, you will do whatever it takes!

I worked there for about a year when my husband came home from a convention and told me he had received a job offer from a company in Chicago. At that time, my husband was a graphic artist and cartographer. I was so excited about moving to Chicago, because I was ready for a new start in a new city and a job that was not as taxing (pun intended). What I did not realize was that I was a workaholic. While at the LA firm, I had worked 16+ hour days during tax season, and had slept on an army cot provided by my husband. Since I lived 55 miles from where I worked, I spent several nights a week on that cot. I thought it was a demanding job that caused me to put work above all else, and not my own desire for excellence and approval.

Once we moved to Chicago, I started looking for another job. I still needed to accumulate my required apprenticeship time to complete my CPA licensing, so I focused on a job at a CPA firm. Because I had some experience, it was much easier to find a job this time.

During our time living in Chicago, seeds of change were planted, and *my* life plan started to stray off *my* intended course. It started with a Mary Kay office party in the fall of 1996. One of the administrative staffers decided to have the party because she had a cousin who was a Mary Kay consultant. Just like any office, all the female staff were invited to the party. I had been using Mary Kay skincare personally for five years. My cousin had gotten me started using the products, but since she lived out of state, I had never attended one of these parties.

As you may have already surmised, I decided to attend. On a humorous note, I was wearing a green jewel toned silk dress, which was not a normal outfit for me, and the consultant wanted me to try an orange lipstick. Even though I did not wear makeup, I told her up front that I knew the color would not work for me, but that I would try it anyways. As expected, it did not work. To this day, orange is not in my color palette.

A few days later the consultant contacted me and asked if I could help her by listening to Mary Kay's marketing and business opportunity information. She was moving up in the company and needed to get opinions from professional business women. I am generally a helpful person, so I agreed.

I remember that snowy November day quite clearly. I was picked up in a pink Cadillac by her sales director and taken to lunch at a local restaurant. They explained how the Mary Kay Company got started, and how it was founded on the principles of God first, family second and career third. They also told me about the different ways consultants could make money. They talked about the ongoing training, and the sisterhood of being in business *for* yourself, but not *by* yourself. They did not know it, but I had several friends and family that had been Mary Kay consultants at one time or another but had gotten out, so I didn't think it worked. Personally, I had prayed for a way to have both a career and a family, because it probably wasn't going to happen as a partner in a CPA firm. Since my mother had been an at-home mom, I felt my only option was to have either a career or a family. Yes, you can have both, but I wanted to be able to spend time with my family, and not watch my children grow up on the other side of a window in a day care center.

Besides the tug of war inside of me concerning my family versus my career, I was considering one obvious challenge of becoming a Mary Kay consultant; I did not wear makeup. I loved the skincare and body care products, but I did not know how to use makeup, and I didn't really want to learn. Also, I did not enjoy the cattiness of women. I think that's why I loved being in a mostly male dominated profession, whereas Mary Kay was comprised almost exclusively of women. Joining Mary Kay also meant I would have to become a sales person. I did not like pushy sales people, and did not want to be known as one. I had a lot of reasons why I did not want to be a sales consultant. Subconsciously though, the idea of "God first, family second and career third" was drawing me towards Mary Kay. But tax season was about to start, and force all other activities to the back burner, so it took a while before I thought seriously about joining Mary Kay again.

After tax season, on April 16, 1997, I received a call inviting me to a Mary Kay career brunch on Saturday, April 26. The 26th is my birthday and I love to celebrate, so I was all in to start the day with a free birthday brunch! I listened to the consultant describe how she was taking care of her aging parents, and how she had the time, money and flexibility to do so because of Mary Kay. She was a top producer in the company and after listening to her story, I mentally substituted the word 'children' for 'aging parents' and left the restaurant that day looking up at the sky, asking God if this was the answer to my prayers.

Have you ever prayed, had an answer come to you, and found that it was not the answer you thought it should be, or maybe it just wasn't wrapped in the gift package you wanted? Looking at it logically, I had too many plans in which Mary Kay did not fit. If I was to become a consultant and pursue it as a full time career, it would mean a total 180 degree shift in both my career and my life.

A few weeks later I attended another Mary Kay event and that is when it clicked. As a CPA, numbers and money *were* my career, so when they announced an offer of a one-time $100 fee, and said you could purchase their products for the rest of your life at 50% off, I took notice. I started calculating how much I had spent during the last year on products and gifts with my consultant, and realized it was worth it even if I only purchased products for me and never sold anything to anyone else. I signed up a few days later, knowing that I would be moving to Atlanta, Georgia in six months.

I was really excited about moving to Atlanta because just like Chicago, I was ready for a new start. Again, I thought my obsession with work was caused by my employer, not me, so changing cities meant a new start. I still didn't realize that I was a workaholic, but that would soon change.

Even though I had signed up as a Mary Kay consultant, I knew that by moving to a new city with few friends or family, it was not wise to jump into Mary Kay full time. My husband was starting his own business, and trying to start up both ventures in a new city did not seem like a wise decision, so I decided to continue working in the accounting field.

This time I chose to go back into corporate accounting. I was blessed with a job very close to our apartment, and began working as a liaison between the accounting and the IT (Information Technology) department for a Y2K system conversion. It became yet another job requiring long hours, because of my need for approval through excellence. Still, this new job allowed me to meet some wonderful people. We formed a group of three, and met weekly to pray for our company, our co-workers, our jobs and our lives. We were from different denominations, but we had one common thread. Jesus was our Savior. This one act of praying regularly with others of faith woke something up inside of me. Slowly, I began to realize that excellence in the eyes of God took priority over excellence on a spreadsheet. My priorities began to change, and my heart changed as well.

The final revelation came when a friend who lives out of state asked me to read about different high maintenance relationships. One of those was called the 'Workhorse'. Suddenly, I realized I was reading about myself. The book had a questionnaire to determine if you were a workhorse or knew one, and I answered "Yes" to every single question. It was a wake-up call.

In addition to working a full time salaried position, I also worked a part-time bookkeeping job. Between both jobs, I don't know how I had time for anything else. I eventually had to ask myself, was I really living or just going through the motions by chasing what I thought was a life?

After processing this workaholic revelation, on December 31, 1999, I told my husband, that I was eventually going to leave my full time job to pursue Mary Kay and my dreams. He was very supportive, but wanted to make certain I thought through the whole transition. He had been self employed, so it was understandable. Looking back on this, I was very thankful that he had been an only child with two working parents, because he knew how to take care of himself. He had done most of the cooking, cleaning, and laundry for these first eight years of marriage.

For the time being, my help was still needed to finish the Y2K conversion. It was not going well. My work hours had been long. I tried to quit multiple times, however, my boss would always persuade me to stay.

Then, on September 1, 2000, I was driving to work, and I distinctly heard a gentle clear voice say, "Turn in your notice today." I knew it was God. I did exactly that, and my boss finally accepted my resignation.

I was excited to start my Mary Kay business full time on October 1. I had a lot of appointments booked for October and November. It was going to be a new life! Then, every single appointment cancelled and would not rebook. I was frustrated, and wondered why God would ask me to leave my old job and not provide success in my new one. I needed income to help pay our household bills. Mary Kay was fun, but it was also my business, and I needed it to bear fruit.

Since things were not working the way I had planned, I told my husband I was going to enjoy my Thanksgiving and Christmas, then get back to work with Mary Kay in January. In all my years of working, I regularly brought work home with me, and simply had not taken the time to enjoy the holidays. I was so totally consumed with work that I could not shut it off. This time, I did. And it was the best Thanksgiving and Christmas I ever had.

While I was working in Atlanta, my husband started his own business and worked at it for several years. One day he was offered a dream job with a Seattle game company as a regional marketing representative for the Southeast region. He loved the job, but had to travel a lot. After being married for eight years and having him home every night, it was a difficult adjustment for both of us. Because of that, I prayed for him to get a job where he did not have to travel. In December 2000, a week before Christmas, my husband's division of the company closed down and he was laid off. That was a wrinkle in my plan that I did not expect, even though I prayed for him to be home instead of traveling.

We both enjoyed our Christmas that year, and I went to work with Mary Kay in January 2001. I decided to put my priorities in order, and I was rewarded with a very nice car, and a promotion to sales director later that year. My husband ended up becoming a school teacher, a desire he'd had for ten years. After that pivotal time, both our lives were never the same.

Interestingly enough, in February 2001, the company I left in October 2000 called to offer me another job. I turned them down. It was nice to have that luxury. Later that Spring, my boss at my former part-time job had lunch with me and asked me this question- "Would you have left your full time job if you knew David was going to be laid off?" I told her there was no way. She said God knew I had to leave my old job first, or I would never have been able to pursue Mary Kay and the dream He had for me. I had to agree.

If twenty years ago someone had told me that I would be a Mary Kay consultant today, I would have been polite, but told them "No way, Jose." The funny thing is that next to my relationship with Jesus and my husband, Mary Kay has been the next best blessing. In the Bible, God's Word says in John 10:27, 'My sheep hear My voice, and I know them, and they follow Me.'

Looking back to my college days, I see that God was trying to talk to me through my father, but my focus was on material things and what I could do to get them, so I didn't listen.

I'm thankful, God, that I heard your gentle, clear voice when you spoke to me directly. You opened my eyes and helped me to put my priorities in order. First, I had to accept Jesus as my Savior and then allow You to become Lord of my life. I set aside my own plans and listened with my heart to the voice of God. What a better life you planned for me and my husband. Thank you so much!!

John J. Myers

John Myers was born May 23, 1955 in Trenton, NJ. He became a ward of the state and was moved to a farm after the early passing of his single mom at just twenty-eight to cancer. Before finishing high school he joined the United States Marine Corps and served in the Third Marine Air Wing during the Vietnam War. Returning from military service, John made his way to Disney World which led to years of success in restaurant management. John has worked with many restaurant chains in Florida and still holds the holiday sales record with one, which with less than one year promoted him to recruiting and training.

In 1989 with no formal training he made the leap to computer

sales and a year later became a system engineer running the computer department of an insurance company which grew from 10 to 150 employees over the next year and half. The next year found him working with Novell, IBM and Microsoft and this major technology brought him to another insurance company. In 1994 he moved to Atlanta, GA, and in 2002 he created his own trillion dollar market place. John J. Myers is now a founding executive with YouLab Global and the CEO and creative force behind www.TheTopMoney.com where he partners with some of the top earners and leaders in the direct sales and marketing industry.

Contact John:

770-896-2300

John@TheTopMoney.com

www.TheTopMoney.com

www.FaceBook.com/TheTopMoney

www.TopMoney.YouLabGlobal.com

John's Voice

A Remarkable Voice

John J. Myers

I watched as 1000 people rushed from the outdoor arena and made their way excitedly to the beach, where the whales were jumping and cavorting in the ocean just a few yards away, lit by the full moon over the Hawaiian sky. I did not move from my seat. My eyes were drawn back toward the stage and I saw him still standing there, still wearing his headset microphone, looking out at the crowd of people who by now were standing on the sandy shore. The crowd was cheering and the roar of the waves coupled with their voices echoed in my ears. I made my way through the maze of chairs and walked to the edge of the platform. He had not seen me coming. I walked up the five steps to the stage, where my movement finally caught his attention. He smiled and stood waiting for me to make my way to the center of the stage. My heart was beating out of my chest, but somehow I heard the sound of a distant seagull, smelled the saltiness of the ocean, and felt the gentle, tropical breeze brush my shirt against my chest. The moment was surreal, and my memory of it is forever etched in my mind as one of the most *remarkable* of my life. I reached out and shook Tony Robbins' hand. He was, and is, the VOICE that changed everything.

My only memory of my mother was when she was in a hospital bed and I was standing next to her saying goodbye. She died of cancer in that hospital room. I must have been about 7-years-old. As I got older, I learned about how I came to live in foster care on a New Jersey farm. According to the couple who owned the farm, my mother was raised an Orthodox Jew and my father was German. My mother's family had disowned her as soon as she married my father.

I was the eldest of three children. I have no memory of my father, but I believe that he left her shortly after my brother was born. There were no family members to take us in, so we three children landed in foster care.

This foster couple had several children of their own, and after my mother died, they fostered the three of us (my brother, my sister and me) along with several other foster children. The foster children worked the farm, and there was a distinct difference in the rules for us and for their biological children. As is typical in the foster care system, children came and went, and along the way I lost track of my sister and brother. I never reconnected with my biological siblings after the last time they left, as there was no reason to. For whatever reason I was one of the children that remained on that farm.

My memories of my childhood are somewhat patchy. I know that this couple was "older" and didn't have the patience that perhaps a younger couple would have had. Their love and attention seemed to be poured only onto their biological children (and grandchildren). There never seemed to be enough money for the foster children.

I remember that I desperately wanted to join the Boy Scouts, and the answer was, as usual, "They don't give us money for that." We ate a lot of peanut butter and jelly sandwiches. When we ran out of jelly we used mustard instead. In spite of the living conditions and abusive behavior, my health was always good, and as an adult I would often joke, "Mustard seeds must be really good for you."

In addition to the mental abuse, there was also physical abuse. The man was surly and muscular. He was a prison guard at a local facility and I remember he was extremely gruff and short-tempered. He had a habit of coming up behind us and grabbing us and, well, beating the hell out of us. There is just no other way to say it. I felt like I always had to watch my back. Once, when I was 16-years-old, he came after me again, but I bolted out the front door and didn't stop running until I was in town. That was when I found out I could run, a talent that I used to my benefit later in life.

Another turning point for me was when I was in 3rd grade. No matter how hard I tried, I just could not read and, as a result, I was "held back." This incident impacted me greatly. I never felt I was smart enough to do much of anything after that, and there was no extra help at home, or even in the school system, to encourage me to believe in myself.

School was quite difficult for me, but I managed to make it through middle school and went on to high school. With no guidance forthcoming, I chose classes that were well beyond my capabilities. I knew that I had never developed the skills required to succeed, so at age 16, I quit school and left the farm, never to return.

I got a job at a local factory doing spot welding, and lived in a rented room. I had dreams, but I knew I couldn't achieve them. I felt lost and hopeless about my future. At 18-years-old, with no high school diploma, no self-confidence and no family, I did what many young men did in that small New Jersey town; I enlisted in the marines. Someone had told me that in the military they would give you a place to sleep, food to eat and job training. I wanted to be trained to do *something*. I wanted to feel I had value. I wanted a future.

The recruitment testing showed that I had an aptitude for mechanical skills, so I was given the position of jet engine mechanic. It sounds quite glamorous, but in reality, it was not. What the marines *did* provide was a place of structure where the rules did not change, and I needed that consistency and direction in my life.

Boot camp was the most difficult part of the program. It was designed to beat us down, and their number one goal was to make us quit. I envisioned the marines as a fulfillment of my dream to be in the Boy Scouts, but I soon found out that this was not child's play. They meant business. I resolved that they would not "beat me", and that I would make it through boot camp. Every day, we lived in fear that we would be dismissed, so I worked very hard to do exactly as I was told. Quite frankly, I had an edge on most of the others, as they had come from loving homes with mothers and fathers who cried when they left. I had left nothing behind and this was my only shot at having a future.

On the morning of graduation, I remember waiting for them to tell me I wasn't going to graduate. I had never completed anything in my life, never excelled at anything, and failed at everything I had ever tried. I fully expected them to pull me out of line and send me away. They didn't. I stood proudly with 11 other young men who had successfully made it through boot camp. We were 12 out of 80. I felt good.

I was stationed in Japan, and the war in Vietnam was still raging. My job was to work on the jet engines of the planes that would take our pilots into battle. I excelled in the marines. I never stood in inspection twice, which means that I was ALWAYS ready for an inspection, and always passed the first time. This was a great achievement few others were able to accomplish. As a result, I began to receive privileges that others did not. I was always at the top of my squad when it came to inspections. I was also the fastest runner on my squad. I would simply flashback to the day when I ran from the man on the farm, and I would outrun everyone else, every single time, which also earned me additional privileges.

I was always the first one on the flight line each morning and the last to leave; I took my service seriously. I had more money than anyone else, because I never spent it on alcohol or cigarettes or any of the extracurricular activities that the other men engaged in during our time off. I was able to purchase a motorcycle with my savings, and on the weekends, I eagerly jumped on it and rode through the countryside. I sometimes stopped in small towns to meet some of the locals, but mostly I enjoyed the scenery and the freedom. I lived like a king during my stay in Japan.

One funny story about my life as a marine involves a morning when I had arrived as usual at the flight line, and hung out a bit waiting for the others to show up. An hour passed and no one joined me. Another hour passed, and I began to panic, wondering what had happened? I truly thought that something terrible had happened and somehow I had missed it.

Eventually, I was relieved to see other men walking toward me, all holding cups of hot coffee. As it turned out, the coffee machine had broken down in the mess hall that morning and they had all stood there, waiting for the machine to be fixed before reporting to the flight line.

I wanted to "sign up" for this life forever. I wanted to stay in Japan and live out my life working on jet engines, but that was not possible, so I eventually left the marines. With nowhere to go, I returned to the only place I knew, that small New Jersey town, but there was nothing there for me.

A friend of mine was heading to Florida to pursue a job, so I made the decision to go with him. The job was in Orlando, so while we were there, we made the trip to Disneyworld. Perhaps it was the magical childhood I had always dreamed of that inspired me, perhaps it was the incredible laughter and positive attitude of the people I met, but I made the decision then and there that I never wanted to leave.

I went from a jet engine mechanic to a busboy at a Disney restaurant. My self-confidence was still lacking, and my skills were more suited to the mechanical world, but I was happy just to be in this environment.

I excelled as a busboy and was promoted to waiter, but I was a horrible at it. My reading and writing skills were challenged, so I got all the orders wrong. I was quickly demoted back to busboy, but the other staff took pity on me and saw my eagerness to learn. After a lot of training and encouragement from my fellow employees, I soon became the best waiter in the restaurant.

I STUDIED people. I began listening to books on self-development. Books like *The Power of Intention* by Wayne Dyer and *Think and Grow Rich* by Napoleon Hill were part of my everyday routine. I struggled to read them, without really comprehending what I read; yet they still made an impact on me.

Eventually, I left Disney after getting recruited away by another major restaurant chain. This move took me from waiter to management, where I took my restaurant from the worst sales performer to the top producer in the entire company.

I always had plenty of money because I never spent it on anything frivolous, and when I wasn't working I loved to explore the cities and beaches. In 1989, I was enjoying a short vacation with a friend in Sarasota, Florida, when I asked the question, "Why would anyone want to live anywhere else in the world?" and immediately made the decision to move there.

After deciding to leave the restaurant business behind, my friend got me an entry-level job in computer sales in Sarasota. I knew nothing at all about computers, but I was willing to learn. I was *eager* to learn. Again, I excelled and became an expert on the subject. Within a short period of time, I was lured away as a consultant for a company who needed my expertise on a major project, and the pay was too good to pass up. What I didn't realize was that this project was scheduled to be completed after one year, and there would be no need for me after it was finished. Once again, I found myself without a job.

I had saved some money, but much of it had been spent on vacations, so I gave myself two weeks to find another job. Although I had seen success in my life, I still had little self-confidence, and my reading and writing skills were a huge problem in the job-hunting process. You must remember, too, that I didn't even have a high school diploma, and going back into the restaurant business was not something I was willing to do. I felt quite hopeless, thinking that I would have to take a low-level job and work my way back up again.

It was very late one evening and I found myself unable to sleep. I was deeply troubled because I had no idea which direction my life was about to go. I knew I wanted more, but I wasn't sure how or where to find it. I turned on the television and watched one of those "infomercials." They were selling a CD series titled, "30 Days to Personal Power," and offered a full refund if I wasn't happy with the results. I purchased it for $399 (a lot of money for me at the time) with the intention of listening to it quickly and returning it.

Within a couple of days of receiving this set of tapes, I realized that I would never return it. The content I heard was nothing less than life-changing, and I knew that I would use the information to land my next career. The CD's were by the personal self-development coach, Tony Robbins.

I knew that if I wanted anything to change in my life, *I* needed to change, and I did. I began intently following the suggestions given on those CD's, listening to them over and over.

During my job hunt, I found an ideal job listing, that of a high-level engineer with a paycheck to match. I was determined to land it. The problem was, I was totally under-qualified for this job, both in education and in job experience, but I did not let that stop me. After listening to the CD's, I felt I was equipped with everything I needed to get that job.

I sent in my application and somehow landed an interview, in spite of my underwhelming resume. The interviewer liked me, but told me point blank that he could not hire me, because I did not have the credentials that were required for the job. In spite of this, I persuaded him to contact the regional office manager and set up an interview for me. I received the same answer. They "liked me," but there was no way the company could invest in me without the required education and job experience. It just wasn't going to happen.

During both interviews, I sat patiently and heard them out. Then I calmly stated, "This is my job. I have decided." It was what I had learned on those CD's that gave me the courage to apply over and over again. I did not give up. I contacted the manager two weeks later, asking about the position. They had not filled it yet. I politely informed him that I knew this would be the case, because the job was mine, and I was just waiting for *them* to figure it out. Several months later, I got the job, and I held that position for nine years. I was very successful, but in 2002 the company shut down.

Around the same time, I was driving by an Indian Reservation and decided to play one of the slot machines. I was not a gambler at all, but after putting a few dollars in one of the machines, I won a nice jackpot of $15,000. After spending it mentally for a couple of days, I began to really think about how to invest this money wisely. I didn't want to waste it. After a bit of contemplation, I decided that I needed to invest in MYSELF, into MY FUTURE. I did the four things that I had resolved to do when I had the time and money-

1. I signed up for a BMW advanced driving school. This was WELL WORTH the investment.

2. I had always had a fear of water, so I took a scuba-diving course and overcame that fear.

3. I always wanted to snow ski, so I took lessons and went on a skiing adventure.

4. I signed up to take all of the available Tony Robbins courses. My thought was, *"If one little set of CD's could help me land a job that I was not qualified for, what would all his seminars and classes do for me?"* The cost for these seminars was about $10,000.

As a result of my Tony Robbins training, I did things that I never dreamed possible, and went on to experience a journey of self-development that few people have the privilege to experience. I took the course titled, "Unleashing the Power Within" and went through the "fire-walking" experience, a true highlight in my life. The fire-walking taught me that I could do anything I set my mind to do. We were in a conference with 1800 people. Tony Robbins told us to focus on what it felt like to walk in wet, dewy grass barefooted, and to think about how it felt for the cold, damp grass to touch the bottom of our feet. I walked the 40-foot long bed of searing, hot coals and never felt a thing!

I had conquered a challenge that few other people can brag about. It was after I returned to work that I realized how incredible the power of my mind could be. Several people asked me if I had burned the bottom of my feet, and I replied that I didn't know; I never looked! I took off my shoes right then and there, only to find that there were no burn marks or blisters. Thinking back, it truly was incredible! After experiencing that, I believed I could do just about anything I set my mind to!

I attended many of his seminars, traveled the country to hear him speak, and grew in character, confidence and determination.

That's when, one incredible evening, I found myself attending a seminar in Hawaii, as Tony Robbins himself took the stage. He had been my mentor and hero from afar. He had trained me and coached me and helped me focus not on where I came from, but where I was going.

That evening, as the whales began to jump and our attention was drawn to the sea, the fickle crowd ran to watch. But I knew that more than anything, I wanted to shake the hand of the man who had so dramatically changed my life. As the others watched the whales, I made my way up to the stage. When the moment came, we shook hands and made small talk. For the life of me I can't remember what we said to each other! I know I handed him my business card, which by now simply read, "REMARKABLE-ONE PERSON—*YOU* CAN MAKE A DIFFERENCE," and I know I said, "Thank you." It was a fleeting moment, one that I'm sure he forgot almost immediately as the whales swam away and the seminar resumed. But, for me, that inspiring moment is forever etched in my memory.

The Voice That Changed Everything—A Book of Gratitude. Thank you, Tony Robbins. You ARE the voice that changed everything, and I am indeed grateful that you helped me find mine.

Diana Lyn Perez

Sales and Networking Strategist, Author and Speaker.
Diana Perez has been the owner of Perez Insurance Pros LLC
for almost 4 years and since December 2014, CEO/Founder of
Business and Balance, Inc. Diana is a seasoned expert at all
things sales and networking. Working in the insurance industry
for over 14 years provided continuous education opportunities,
Sales training & success as well as personal growth. Ms. Perez
has worked for the #1 world risk insurance brokers Marsh and
McLennan among other high-end insurance brokers. Combined
with her vast knowledge and the burning desire to elevate others in the community, Ms Perez' skills and mindset afforded

her the ability and expertise to
generate a massive growth in
sales in premiums in excess of
$10,000 for many of her clients in
the affluent market. Continuously
educating herself, she has become
a business and insurance expert
to many clients, friends and networking partners.

Diana found great passion in
connecting with women, helping

them grow by providing expert advice and training on how to balancing business with fun and rest. Since its founding in December 2014, Business & Balance Ladies of Atlanta (BBLA) has grown to over 2,300 ladies through her Facebook group platform in just 9 months! Lastly, with hundreds of clients and members attending her events, classes and monthly meetings, Ms Perez' efforts are regarded by many as a phenomenal improvement in the Atlanta business market. Ms. Perez offers regular strategy sales & networking sessions, workshops for professionals and business owners as well as powerful empowerment and teaching events. This networking entrepreneur organization is unlike any other in Georgia.

Contact Diana
www.businessandbalance.org
Email
diana@businessandbalance.org

Diana's Voice

Hold on...Hold on to That Voice

Diana Lyn Perez

C an you hear that sweet, soft, loving whisper? "Precious child of mine, listen. What you feel is NOT the sum total of what is to COME."

As the door slams, LOUDLY, I hear something different. I am scared. I am lost. I want OUT! How can this be happening to her? Not the one woman who has spoken such loving, encouraging and motivating words to me. She has taken care of me, greatly.

Why has this happened? Why HER, God!? Why, ME!?

I hear GOD speak, "Why *not* you, Diana? I have a great and unbelievable journey for you. Listen to Me. Hear my Holy Spirit. Focus. Focus on Me!"

BOOM, BANG, HIT after HIT, PUNCH after PUNCH. SCREAMS!

Lord, HELP us!

She walks out of the bedroom, tears overflowing from her beautiful eyes. I see some blood. I see swelling and scratches. My sweet mother, what has he *done* to you?

I hear my younger brother, David, crying out loud. Wanting her to pick him up from his crib.

Evelyn, my mother, my beautiful, strong, woman of God, unconditional lover of all. Watching him hit, smack and curse you, I have to hide in the corner, at just 6 years old, and ask God to PLEASE rescue us! He doesn't. Well, not yet, anyway. The abuse goes on for a year. The black eyes, the bruising and the yelling. Day by day, it is what she and I must endure. The thought of her pain brings me to my knees, weeping for her. Praying.

You see, my mother, although a woman of immense courage and strength, took punch after punch from this man who said he loved her. He didn't love her. Even at a young age, *I* knew that. He wouldn't hurt her if he did. He had moved us from all that was familiar. We lived in a new area and I attended a new school. I was not able to leave the house, unless it was to go to my new "grandmother's" house. She was a sweet lady, but I didn't want to be anywhere near this man. I was locked up, not allowed to leave the house.

Am I an animal? Why does he keep us so hidden? Why can't he see what I see in her? If he did, he would know that what he is doing is the worst thing any child, or person for that matter, could ever endure.

It's time to shower. My mother comes in to help me. She turns me around to gently wash my backside. I begin to daydream, thinking of my older sister, Melissa. We had to leave her in New York with my grandmother. The man didn't want "her." I didn't understand why. My sister was beautiful, the prettiest girl I thought ever existed. Everyone, friends and family, loved her. More importantly, I loved her, her skin color an almond shade of perfection, her smile SO engaging. I'm daydreaming of the day I get to see my sister again, to play with her again.

Suddenly, I hear my mother raise her voice and interrupt my dream, "What happened, Diana!? Why do you have this bruise on your backside?"

I have no words. I sit in silence. Head bowed. She screams! She runs in the bedroom where he is, and I hear banging and loud screaming again.

"Mom, please! Not for my sake!" It didn't matter; I was her child. She had to do something, so she did! But, at the expense of the horrendous beating she takes at the same time.

I remember: He had lifted me in the air and yelled at me earlier that morning. For what, I can't recall; I was a young child. Maybe I didn't clean something up. Maybe I was a bad girl. BOOM!!!!!! I hit the ground, and *very* hard! He just *threw* me! It hurts, the pain.

Why us, Lord?

"Focus, Diana. Focus on My love. There is no greater love than that of your Father God! I will take the pain away. You have a greater journey ahead. Hold on."

"God is our refuge and strength, an ever-present help in trouble" (Psalm 46:1, NIV).

My mother, still screaming..."Don't. You. EVER! Put your hands, on *my* child!!"

BOOM!! Another smack to her face!

"Please, stop! I am OK! I am OK!" I plead.

After a few minutes, she returns to the bathroom. I am still soaking in the tub, fearing for my life *and* hers.

"I'll never let anyone hurt you. You are my child. You are beautiful and smart and I love you, Diana. We will get out of here. Mommy loves you!"

Several days later, it's early in the morning. I am getting ready for school. I am so excited. Excited to get out of this house. My new teacher, with the biggest smile, welcomes me with open arms.

Can't she see? I think. *Can't she see I am hurting, I am in pain? I need help; we need help.*

I won't dare tell her. All I want is to stay out of that house. I want my mom here, safe and by my side.

I hear on the overhead speaker, "Diana Perez's mother is here to pick her up early!"

OH JOY!!!!! I am thrilled to see my Mom. How I love her, standing in the office, her black eye as shiny as it was when he gave it to her.

"Hi, Mom!!!!!! What are you doing here? Am I in trouble? Are you OK? Where is little David, my brother?"

"Diana just come with me."

Beside her, I see my Aunt Gloria. We call her Tita (THI-TA).
"Hi Tita!"

"Hi, sweetie," she says. "How are you?"

I just look at her. I have no words. My mom signs me out of school. We get into the hallway.

I ask her, loudly, "Where are we going? What is going on Mom?"

"Diana, Listen to me." She gets down to eye level. "We are leaving."

"Leaving? Where are we going? Who are we going with? Where is little David?"

"He is home, Diana. Diana, listen. I told you, I was getting us out of here didn't I?"

"Yes, Mom! You did. But what about David?"

"His father has told me before if I ever, *ever*, take his son from him he will kill us ALL. I will come back for David! I *will* come back for my son."

"But, Mom, where are we going?"

"We are running away."

"Mom, we are running from him?"

"YES! Let's go. Right now!"

An overwhelming amount of fear comes over me. *Wait, aren't I supposed to be happy?* I think to myself.

"NO, he will find us. Mom, he will find us!"

"No, he won't Diana; it is OVER! I. Love. You." Her words rang in my ear and penetrated my heart.

I am crying, I am happy. I feel JOY like none I have ever felt in my life. At that moment, I knew things would be okay. But, I am worried for my little brother. I love him.

"Focus, Diana. Listen to Me." I remember, I heard God say, "I have a GREAT and unbelievable journey for you. Focus on Me." *Thank You, GOD!*

He gives strength to the weary and increases the power of the weak. Even the youthful grow tired and weary, and young men stumble and fall; but those who hope in the Lord will renew their strength. They will soar on wings like eagles, they will run and not grow weary, they will walk and not be faint. (Isaiah 40: 29-31, NIV)

Within an hour, we are pulling into a strange community.

"Where are we, Mom?"

As we pull up to this community, it looks dirty outside. The buildings are brick. The stairs are metal. The windows are broken in some of the apartments. I see some children playing. *Maybe they will play with me,* I think.

Up the stairs we climb. I am very happy once the door opened. I am greeted by my "Aunt" Susy.

"Hi! Aunt Sue Mae!!" I say so joyfully. "Are we staying here with you?"

"Yes, Baby, you are!" Aunt Sue Mae says.

"Thank You, GOD!" I whisper.

I am with my extended family—they are really just some great friends of my mom—my "cousins." Tita and everyone are around, talking. I begin playing with my cousin Suiwava. I hear my mother from the living room, telling them what she did, how she has had enough!

"No man is going to beat MY child. Beat ME! NEVER my child."

"Or you either, Mom," I whisper.

There she sits, this woman of extreme courage. She has left him. The monster is gone. No more beatings, no more crying, no more screaming and no more hiding in the corner. No more looking out of the window, hoping to be saved. I have been set free! *Thank You, GOD!*

In everything, we must give thanks! (1 Thessalonians 5:18)

Later, when I was a teenager, my mother and I were at a local gas station. When we returned to the car, my mother and I noticed a car that had pulled up behind ours, blocking us from pulling out. Before she could open our locks, a man jumped out of the car. I watch the unfolding scene and, with a rush of fear, I saw it was *him*. I asked my mom if she wanted me to run inside the store and tell them to call the police.

She said, "No, be calm..."

He walked up to mom. "You thought you wouldn't ever see me again. You were wrong, Evelyn," he sneered. "Get in the car!"

My mother did not respond to his direct, harsh and scary voice. Calmly, she asked, "Where is my son?"

"Don't worry about him." he said.

She continues, "I want to see him. One day, I will explain to my son what has happened. God will see it happen."

He laughed an evil, terrifying laugh.

My mother stood, poised with such grace, strength and calmness—I now know it was God, through His Holy Spirit, giving her calmness and strength—and because of her faith, she told him, "I am getting in my car and leaving. Move your car or I will back right into it!"

She instructed me to get in the car and I did. She turned the car on and revved the engine. He got into his car and hurried to move. We never saw him again.

He never found us, just as Mom had promised, but for years I struggled in life because of trust issues with men, and people in general.

To help me fight my distrust and to grow in my faith, Mom continued to pour into me daily. "Diana you are beautiful. Forget what others have to say. You are unique! God has given you all you need to be great. I will always be here for you, to love and protect you. So, be great, love others and do good!" She hugged me when I needed it, and scolded me when it was good for me. "Make me proud," she would say.

So I am. My constant goal: Make Mom Proud. I *vowed* to honor her, and make her proud.

The strength of my mother, her undeniable strength, reminds me every day of how she was, and is, the Proverbs 31 woman.

This situation, this traumatic life-changing situation, made me determined that no matter who or what may come my way, I would always push forward in life with the tenacity and drive that triathletes must carry when they run the race of their life.

So must you, dear reader, *push forward*. Push until you have no breath left. When you see a challenge, let it motivate you to overcome it. Once you overcome it, remember my mother's actions. Be calm and steady. Remember your GOD-given, immeasurable strength and, most importantly, God's words…Focus on Him!

I grew up in a bad neighborhood, and I watched my absolutely amazing mother, Evelyn, work what seemed to be 70 hours a week. Yet, she still, so graciously, made sure my sister and I had all of our needs met.

With no college education, though, I believe everyone should get trained if they don't get a opportunity to finish school and educated in a profession or skill set to be effective, I opened my first business in 2012. It grew quickly, both because of the skills I obtained by working hard, my networking, and because I truly have a servant's heart.

I was able to live very comfortably off of the income from my first business, but it could never compare to the greatness of finding my true passion: Passing on to other women all that I received from my mother's teaching, and sharing her work ethic and tenacity—and the truth of God's Word manifested through true miracles in my life.

So, I created Business & Balance, Inc., a professional women's organization where we provide women the platform and resources to cultivate a successful personal and business life. I am full of joy, not from receiving, but from giving. Giving what only GOD has given unto me. I *am* holding on, holding onto GOD's voice and my mother's love. I am pressing on past the challenges, the naysayers and the hurdles, with GOD's help, and allowing Him to continue to mold me into the woman *He* wants me to be.

I was made for such a journey as this!

You, too, are made and built in strength! Remember, you are a precious, special and creative being. Hold onto *that* Voice... God bless you!

Afterword

The Voice That Changed Everything—A Book of Gratitude

In the preparing of this book collaboration, one common thread continued to surface as our co-authors began writing their chapters, the act of giving gratitude, of saying "Thank You", gave all of us a sense of great satisfaction, and in identifying our VOICES, it was evident that there were many others to thank along the way!

Carol Neal and I believe that we have created a fantastic opportunity to show gratitude in a monumental way—through this book series that will continue to grow in depth and momentum as people around the world are inspired to reach for their own greatness, to walk in the destiny that God has designed for them!

There are so many ways to show gratitude, and yet, in our busy life, our busy world, we quite often fail to stop and make sure we have properly thanked those people in our lives that made a real difference. Showing gratitude opens the door to the miraculous; whatever we are grateful for, we attract more of in our lives.

We hope that you will consider saying "Thank You" to your "Voice That Changed Everything" by writing a chapter in an upcoming volume of our book series.

We hope that our authors have inspired *you* to "*be the Voice*" that changes everything for someone else—a co-worker, your children, your spouse, your friend.

We love the "30-Day Gratitude Challenge" which was mentioned by one of our authors, given by Kody Bateman, CEO and Founder of Send-Out Cards—that is, send a card of gratitude to someone every day for 30 days and 'see what happens'! When you SEND words of gratitude, you will RECEIVE so much! (To learn more about the 30-Day Gratitude Challenge, go to www.sendoutcards.com/BeTheVoice or contact me at Tracee@ TraceeRandall.com.)

You can also contact me to receive information about how to be part of an upcoming volume, or to learn more about our "Be The Voice" Workshops and events. If you know of anyone who would like to be considered as a co-author for a future book, have them email us!

Thank you for sharing this book series with others who will be inspired and changed! Carol and I are *grateful* for YOU, our readers!

Tracee Randall
Contact me at Tracee@TraceeRandall.com

CPSIA information can be obtained
at www.ICGtesting.com
Printed in the USA
FFOW03n0509030116
19799FF